THE SOCIOLOGY OF SUBCULTURES

THE GLENDESSARY PRESS — *BERKELEY*

Consulting Editor:

Donald A. Hansen *University of California, Berkeley*

The SOCIOLOGY

of SUBCULTURES

edited by

David O. Arnold

University of California
Santa Barbara

FOREWORD

Since about 1960, American academic circles have been flooded with papers and conversations heavily laced with the word "subculture." Although the new *International Encyclopedia of the Social Sciences* does not mention this concept, it has spread to the outside world. Judges are dismissing offenders on the ground that their alleged criminal offense was "subcultural," social workers are up to their ears in studies of "subcultural differences," and even *Time* magazine occasionally sprinkles its pages with the term.

Sociologists, especially those interested in delinquency and crime, have in the last decade devoted an overwhelming amount of time, money and energy to studies of how "subcultures" arise, persist, and change. The time has come to point out, as this book does, that the results of these studies are not cumulative, in a scientific sense. This is evident from the fact that usage of the subculture concept varies from one in which "gang" and "subculture" are used as synonyms to one in which the "sub" in "subculture" is taken to mean "inferior." The confusion has arisen in part because so few persons have bothered to explore the history of the concept, or tried to show its relationship to other concepts and theories that help make sense of the seemingly chaotic mess that sociologists and social psychologists call social structure and social process.

But the book does more than show that all is not well. It presents an interactionist, process, model of subcultures which combines some ideas about social structure and some ideas about differential social interaction. The model certainly will not be the last word on the subject, but it rightfully defines "the problem" in researchable terms. In sociological studies, much wheel-spinning has occurred as structural theorists have had to pause and rediscover the interaction processes identified as crucial many years ago by process theorists such as Baldwin, Cooley, Dewey, and Mead.

The study of subcultures needs to be integrated with studies of the legal process. Perhaps the norms of the criminal law are what people have in mind when they refer to "conventional culture," "dominant culture," and "culture." And perhaps, then, "subculture" is just a way of saying—somewhat abusively—that some classes of persons often violate the law. (I have yet to hear the military-industrial complex called a "subculture.")

Among the characteristics of the legal process are discrepancies between the moral norms of the lawmakers and the moral norms of the persons to whom the laws are to apply. The "positional norms" surrounding class status, sex status, age status, health status, ethnic status, and family status, among others, distinguish persons in terms of rights, privileges, duties, and prestige. In short, these positional norms are moral norms which define expectations for conduct. But law norms are peculiar, as compared with these positional norms, in such aspects as specificity, harm, intent, punishment, process of change, and process of enforcement. They are "universal" rules which ought to be followed by everyone except the insane and the very young. They differ from moral norms, which recommend but do not require certain courses of conduct.

Conflicts between positional norms get "resolved" in the legislative process, but such "resolution" does not mean that the ensuing law norms are subscribed to uniformly or universally. While the normative expectations within a society vary with the structural conditions of class, sex, ethnicity, etc., the expectations and requirements of the criminal law do not allow for this variability. A system of similarities based on status differentiation, then, is likely to be called a "subculture" simply because it varies from the system of similarities codified in the law. The norms of class position, in fact, allow for implementation, in the penal law, of the norms of the powerful. Accordingly, as power shifts, different positional norms get incorporated into the law norms, creating further "subcultures."

To put the matter in another way, normative conflict is inherent in social structure. The conflicts of relevance to delinquency, crime, and deviance are those in which the choices available to a person—because of one or more of his positions in the social structure—are inappropriate to the choices that the law norms demand that he make. To take a simple example, it is apparent that young persons and Negroes do not have the degree of access to the lawmaking process that is available to middle-aged whites. Consequently, juvenile crime and Negro crime are in many respects expressions of a condition of conflict between the positional norms of age and ethnicity and the norms of the white adult lawmakers whose positional norms get codified in the laws as universals. A "solution" to the dilemma arising from this system of creating our own "deviants" is to label the youth norms and the ethnic norms as "subcultures" which should be studied and controlled.

As to the history reported in Part I, I have a hunch that the ecological studies of Shaw and McKay, in which the concept "delinquency area" was used, had some effect on Sutherland's later use of the "behavior system" concept. Perhaps it also led, somehow, to the more widely used "subculture" idea. Further, Thorsten Sellin's 1938 monograph (*Culture Conflict and Crime*) had in it most of the means-goals arguments that are now so popular in discussions of subcultures.

Santa Barbara, California   **Donald R. Cressey**
August 18, 1969

CONTENTS

III SUBCULTURE THEORY

IV RECENT FORMULATIONS

THE SOCIOLOGY OF SUBCULTURES

INTRODUCTION

During the last decade the concept "subculture" emerged to take a place with such terms as "social class," "role," and "function," as one of sociology's most basic tools. But it is a tool not yet well used. When we study social classes in contemporary America we start by examining the classic works of men such as Warner, Marx, Weber, and perhaps even Plato and Aristotle. Not so when we study subcultures. It is as if the accelerated use of the concept has caught us unawares. We examine Mexican-American subcultures, middle-class subcultures, or subcultures of organized crime as if they were wholly unrelated to earlier ideas developed in studies of other subcultures. As a consequence subculture research has not been as cumulative as it might have been. One purpose of the present volume is to correct this deficiency by presenting in a single place various formulations of subculture previously scattered and in some cases unknown or forgotten.

Although only one of the "classic" formulations of subculture which appear in Part I of this book deals with criminal, delinquent, or any other sort of deviant subcultures, most sociologists today seem to think that subculture analysis is useful only to students of deviant behavior. Actually its value extends to most, perhaps all, of the subfields of sociology. Furthermore, it can be useful not only to these various subfields, but to the parent discipline as well. Although we have paid a great deal of attention to "theories of the middle range," we have not worried about what might be termed *data* of the middle range. Instead we have macrosociology, which bites off pieces of data so large that even in the best of hands analysis is usually superficial and sloppy. And we have microsociology, which bites off pieces so small that after one is analyzed we likely are at a loss for some place to put it, some way to link it to broader sociological concerns.

Subcultures, deviant or not, allow us to gather data in pieces small enough to be subjected to systematic analysis, yet large enough to be of clear theoretical and practical importance. Subcultures are worth knowing about in their own right. (By "knowing" I mean understanding, having an adequate explanation for, not just being somewhat familiar with, describing.) But subcultures may also be viewed as total cultures in miniature, and thus serve as laboratories for developing theories that account for the activities of total societies.

Thomas Lasswell recently pointed out that:

> ... *every group that is at all functional must have a culture of its own that is somewhat similar to the cultures of other groups with whom it interacts. Such a group culture is not partial or miniature, it is a complete, full-blown set of beliefs, knowledges, and ways for adjustment to the physical and social environment.*[1]

Lasswell goes on to say that while "... the culture itself is not 'smaller' than the great culture ... the group which enacts it is smaller than the great society."[2] Thus the study of subcultures is a more manageable task than the study of the total culture of a complex society, yet many of the findings of subculture studies may be generalizable to the larger cultures.

By now the reader may feel that I am ignoring the distinction between society and culture, and that perhaps this will be followed by a corresponding indifference to the distinction between subsociety (or group or population segment) and subculture. This is indeed the case. Most introductory textbooks in sociology define society so that it excludes culture, and culture so that it excludes society, thereby painlessly (or perhaps not so) doubling the student's sociological vocabulary. Yet by the fourth chapter the author usually forgets the distinction and uses the terms interchangably. "Culture" refers to ideas. "Society" refers to people. Our ultimate concern is usually with what these people do, with their behavior. Most often we subsume this under discussions of society, although it is not infrequently slipped into a consideration of culture. Sometimes we just talk in a sort of limbo, blithly ignoring the society-culture boxes we so painstakingly constructed. Any intelligent description of a collection of people, what they do and think and why they do and think as they do must necessarily employ both societal and cultural concepts, as well as behavioral. Thus we find that sociologists who talk about "subcultures" and those who talk about "behavior systems," and in some cases those who talk about "communities," "reference groups," etc., are really concerned with much the same range of phenomena. Our treatment of the phenomena should be as systematic as possible; our labels for it need be systematic only insofar as this aids rather than gets in the way of that central concern.

Fifty years ago only slight attention was paid to social class in the teaching of sociology, but today virtually every college and university offers one or more courses on the subject, and additional time is spent on it in other courses. Such is not yet the case with subculture. Therefore, in contrast to the most widely-assigned book in stratification courses—which runs close to 700 double-column pages in length and costs approximately ten dollars—this book was intended to be less weighty, in order to serve as supplementary reading in a variety of courses. Thus, two sorts of compromises were required. First, many articles that are relevant to the subject had to be excluded, and second, the articles that were included had to be edited. I hope that the editing has not substantially altered the thrust of any of these articles. As for the excluded articles, I have listed a few of the most important in a bibliography at the end of the book, and urge the reader to take the trouble to look them up. I also hope that this volume will contribute to the growth of subculture research and subculture theory in sociology, so that in a few more years there will be courses devoted entirely to this area. When this occurs perhaps it will be feasible to publish books on subculture that are exhaustive rather than suggestive.

The chapters of this book are grouped into four parts. Part I presents the earliest systematic formulations of subculture as a sociological concept; part IV presents some of the more recent formulations. Parts II and III deal with specific but crucial sub-topics of subculture research. Part II asks what the boundaries of these systems we term subcultures look like. Does each subculture stand alone, or do they overlap each other? How are subcultures in a society related to the culture of that society? What is the relationship between individuals and subcultures? Part III asks how subcultures come into existence, how they change, and how they affect the individuals who come into contact with them.

In all, these articles should offer an informed overview of a critical area of sociology that has too long remained vague in the words and works of all but a few sociologists.

FOOTNOTES
[1]Thomas Lasswell, *Class and Stratum,* Boston: Houghton Mifflin (1965), 211.
[2]*Ibid.,* 212.

Part One

EARLY
FORMULATIONS

Although Green made passing use of "subculture" in 1946, attention first focused on this term in Milton Gordon's article, "The Concept of the Sub-culture and its Application," originally published in 1947 and appearing here as Chapter Three. But in studying the notion of subculture it is important to not equate the term with the idea. Looking for the latter, whether labeled subculture or not, we find it first in 1939, in a chapter titled "Behavior Systems in Crime," in the third edition of Edwin Sutherland's Principles of Criminology. *The overlap between behavior system and subculture is made clear by Sutherland's definition of his concept:*

> . . . a behavior system in crime . . . includes, in addition to the individual acts, the codes, traditions, *esprit de corps,* social relationships among the direct participants, and indirect participation of many other persons. It is thus essentially a groupway of life.

Later editions of Principles of Criminology *(now co-authored by Sutherland and Donald R. Cressey,) have elaborated this concept, but it is the original 1939 formulation which is reprinted as Chapter One of the present volume. In an article that appeared a few months later, A. B. Hollingshead generalized Sutherland's notion of behavior systems, and argued that ". . . the sociologist and anthropologist should include within the focus of their attention the behavior systems of definable functional groups," wherever they occur, whether criminal or not. Hollingshead's discussion appears here as Chapter Two. Whereas the main concern of Chapter Two is with occupational subcultures (Hollingshead does mention ethnic subcultures at one point), Chapter Three, by Gordon, is concerned with the subcultures of broader segments of the population. Thus we have the seminal but rather restricted formulation by Sutherland, and the extensions by Hollingshead and Gordon which set the stage for the present-day study of subculture.*

1

BEHAVIOR SYSTEMS IN CRIME

Edwin H. Sutherland

INTRODUCTION

Most of the scientific work in criminology has been directed at the explanation of crime in general. Crime in general consists of a great variety of criminal acts. These acts have very little in common except the fact that they are all violations of law. They differ among themselves in the motives and characteristics of the offenders, the characteristics of the victims, the situations in which they occur, the techniques which are used, the damages which result, and the reactions of the victims and of the public. Consequently it is not likely that a general explanation of all crimes will be sufficiently specific or precise to aid greatly in understanding or controlling crime. In order to make progress in the explanation of crime it is desirable to break crime into more homogeneous units. In this respect crime is like disease. Some general theories of disease have been stated and are useful. The germ theory of disease is a very useful general theory, but even this theory does not apply to all diseases. Progress in the explanation of disease is being made principally by the studies of specific diseases. Similarly, it is desirable to concentrate research work in criminology on specific crimes.

What, for purposes of theoretical explanation, is a specific crime? Evidently it is not a crime as legally defined, for almost any one of the legally defined crimes involves a great variety of casual processes. Jerome Hall has shown this excellently in the field of larceny from the point of view of control, and has suggested a classification of larcenies into sociological units.[1] Such a sociological unit or entity may be called a behavior system.

THE BEHAVIOR SYSTEM IN CRIME

The behavior system in crime may be described by its three principal characteristics. First, a behavior system in crime is not merely an aggregation of individual criminal acts. It is an integrated unit, which includes, in addition to the individual acts, the codes, traditions, *esprit de corps,* social relationships among the direct participants, and indirect participation of many other persons. It is thus essentially a groupway of life. Behavior systems in crime may be illustrated by professional theft, circus grifting, drug addiction racketeering, fraudulent advertising, and manipulation of corporate securities as practised by Insull, the Van Sweringens, and many others.

Second, the behavior which occurs in a behavior system is not unique to any particular individual. It is common behavior. It operates in the same manner in a large number of persons and therefore it should be possible to find causal factors and processes which are not unique to the particular individual.

Third, while common and joint participation in the system is the essential characteristic of a behavior system, it can frequently be identified by the feeling of identification of those who participate in it. If the participants feel that they belong together for this purpose, they do belong together. A professional confidence man and a professional forger would feel that they belonged together, even though they used different technique, because they have many common interests and standards and can therefore participate in the same system. On the other hand an embezzler would not identify himself with an automobile thief. If these two should meet they would have no common reactions or sentiments growing out of their crimes except such as were common to practically all other persons who violate the laws. Ultimately a behavior system should be defined as a way of life which grows out of a unified causal process. A behavior system in this respect would be similar to a disease, which is differentiated from other diseases by the causal process common to it regardless of the person in whom it occurs.

If a behavior system can be isolated, the problem is to explain that system as a unit. This is similar to an attempt to explain baseball in America. This does not consist primarily of explaining why a particular person becomes a baseball player, and in fact the explanation of why a particular person becomes a ball player merely assumes the existence and persistence of baseball as a system. By taking the behavior system as a problem it is possible to avoid some of the methodological difficulties which arise when the act of a specific person is taken as the problem.

Moreover, by taking the behavior system as the problem it is possible to break away from the legal limitations that have often impeded scientific work in criminology. A sociological unit need not be confined to the legal proscriptions. It can be studied wherever it exists, whether as crime or not crime, and generalizations should apply throughout the system. In this way the criminologist can define his own units and does not need to accept the decisions of courts and legislatures. . . .

PROFESSIONAL THEFT AS A BEHAVIOR SYSTEM

Professional theft is presented as an illustration of a behavior system which can be defined and explained as a unit.

The principal, but not the only, rackets used by professional thieves are confidence games, shoplifting, and pocket-picking. Not all persons who commit these specific crimes are professional thieves. Professional thieves make a regular business of theft. They use techniques which have been developed over a period of centuries and transmitted to them through traditions and personal association. They have codes of behavior, *esprit de corps,* and consensus. They have a high status among other thieves and in the political and criminal underworld in general. They have differential association in the sense that they associate with each other and not, on the same basis, with outsiders, and also in the sense that they select their colleagues. Because of this differential association they develop a common language or argot which is relatively unknown to persons not in the profession. And they have organization. A thief is a professional when he has these six characteristics: regular work at theft, technical skill, consensus, status, differential association, and organization. The amateur thief is not a professional; neither is the consistently dishonest bondsalesman. The case is not quite so clear for the professional burglar or robber, for there the principal differential is the nature of the technique and the identification. The techniques of the professional thief are much the same as those of the salesman and the actor; they consist of methods of manipulating the interests, attention, and behavior of the victim. The professional thief depends on cleverness and wits, while the robber or burglar resorts more frequently to force or threat of force. Professional thieves have their groupways of behavior for the principal situations which confront them in their criminal activities. Consequently professional theft is a behavior system and a sociological entity.

The principal genetic question regarding professional theft is, How does it originate and how is it perpetuated in our culture? A secondary question is, How does a particular person get into this professional group?

The motives of professional thieves are much the same as the motives of other occupational groups: they wish to make money in safety. These desires require no specific explanation. The specific problem is, How do professional thieves remain secure in their violations of the law? Many professional thieves have conducted their illegal activities for a normal lifetime and never been locked up longer than a few days at a time; others have had one or two terms over a period of twenty or thirty years.

Security in professional theft is attained in three ways. First, the thieves select rackets that involve a minimum of danger. The confidence game is relatively safe because the victim generally agrees to participate in a dishonest transaction and when he finds that he is the victim he cannot make complaint without disgracing himself. Shoplifting is relatively safe because stores do not wish to run the risk of accusing legitimate customers of stealing, and the professional shoplifter makes it a point to look and act like a legitimate customer. Picking pockets is relatively safe because the legal rules of evidence require direct evidence that the thief puts his hand in the pocket and withdraws money, and that evidence is seldom secured. Second, the professional thieves develop clever and skilled techniques for executing the crimes which they select. They do this through tradition, tutelage, and general association. Third, they make arrangements to fix those cases in which they may be caught. Because of the importance of "the fix" in the profession of theft it will be discussed in more detail.

The professional thief expects to fix every case in which he may be caught. He generally does not fix the case himself but employs a professional fixer, for in a larger city one man generally does all of the fixing for all of the professional thieves. Whether the fixing is done by the thieves themselves or by their fixer, it is generally accomplished by the direct or indirect payment of money. First, a promise is made to the victim that his stolen property will be returned, sometimes with a bonus, if he will refuse to push the prosecution or to testify in a way that would damage the thief. A large proportion of the cases are fixed in this manner, for the victim is generally more interested in the return of his stolen property than he is in seeing that justice is done to the thieves. Second, the police, prosecutor, bailiff, or judge may be bribed. The policeman may advise the victim to take his money back and not be bothered with a long trial; or he may give evidence which conflicts with that of the victim or other witnesses; or he may render other services. The prosecutor may refuse to push the prosecution or, if he is compelled to do so, he may make a very weak effort to bring out evidence which is damaging to the thief. As a last resort, the judge may be bribed to render decisions in favor of the thief, or he may impose minor penalties. It is not necessary that everyone of these office-holders act dishonestly. The only thing necessary is to find one of them who will twist or pervert evidence or decisions. Most of the cases are fixed before they reach the higher courts. They can be fixed more easily in municipal courts than in federal courts. But a federal judge who presided at an important trial of confidence men has recently been indicted for accepting indirect bribes from persons and firms whose cases were heard in his court.

The profession of theft, then, exists in modern society because victims are more interested in getting their property back than in abstract justice, because officeholders are under the control of a political machine or have predatory personal interests. Also, professional theft exists because business concerns are willing to purchase stolen commodities, and because lawyers are willing to defend professional thieves by every clever argument and device available. Professional theft exists not only because persons are willing to steal, but also because the rest of society does not present a solid front against theft. In other words, society is disorganized with reference to theft.

The entrance of a particular person into the professional group is of secondary importance, for the explanation of theft as a profession cannot be found in the life-history of one of the members of the profession. Rather it is necessary to understand the profession in order to explain the individual thief. For admission into the profession is not merely an act of will of a person who decides that he would like to be a professional thief. He can no more become a professional thief in that manner than he can become a professional ballplayer. Others must permit him to become a professional thief, just as they must permit a person to become a professional ball-player. Members of the profession make their entrance by a process of mutual selection.

No one can acquire all of the skills and work safely in co-operation with others without training and tutelage. Tutelage can be given only by those already in the profession. Consequently one gets into the profession by acceptance. The neophyte is instructed verbally regarding the principles of the racket and regarding the simple part he is given to play in it. He performs these minor tasks under the supervision of the professional thieves. If he does these tasks satisfactorily his responsibilities may be increased until he is finally given the same tasks as regular members of the profession. Not only is he instructed in the execution of the crime, but also in the codes of behavior; and he is made acquainted with other thieves, with the fixer, and the fences. This personal acquaintance is necessary for a safe career in the underworld.

Professional thieves do not extend this tutelage to everyone who would like to join them. They extend their assistance, of course, only to those with whom they come in contact in a friendly manner; that is, to fellow-lodgers in hotels, rooming-houses, or jails, and to waiters, cashiers, and taxicab drivers. The thieves get acquainted with most of these people in a legitimate manner, and confidence develops. They like a certain prospect, and he likes them. They may suggest that he join them, but more frequently he asks to join them because he wants more money than he can make at legitimate work and because their life looks attractive. Doubtless thousands of others with whom they do not come in contact in this manner have the abilities required for professional theft, but they do not happen to meet. Thus entrance into the profession is by selection. The selection is impersonal in the sense that a person must be in a position where he will come in contact with professional thieves in order to develop personal acquaintance. The selection is also personal in the sense that the thieves must be attracted to the prospect, and he must be attracted to them. He has a veto on joining the profession, but just as certainly they have a veto on him joining it.[2]

CIRCUS GRIFTING

Circus grifting is a second behavior system in crime, which will be described as an illustration of this method of analysis. It consists principally of sure-thing gambling, as seen in the shell-game, three-card monte, the eight-dice cloth, the cologne joint, and the spindle. In order that circus grifting may be conducted satisfactorily and safely, four elements are necessary: grifters, victims, a dishonest circus management, and dishonest public officials. The behavior system is a combination of these four elements.

Circus grifters come from two principal sources. They may have been grifting previously in state fairs, resort communities, or carnivals, with methods somewhat similar to those used in the circus. Or they may have been living in the community in which the circus is playing, have been employed for a day as a shill or assistant in one of the games, have proved efficient, and have been taken along with the circus and trained in other details of the game. It is reported that a large proportion of the circus grifters originated in Indiana, where several circuses make their winter headquarters.

The circus grifters form a relatively cohesive group. They have a saying, "Once a circus grifter, always a circus grifter." The gambling games played in the circus are played elsewhere, but seldom with the same abandon. Many people who play one of these games elsewhere do not succeed in the circus, and many who are very successful in the circus are inefficient when they try to operate the same games elsewhere. The grifters in a particular circus are a somewhat exclusive group while the circus is on the road; the performers do not associate with them. In the early days the grifters rode in the "privilege car" of the circus train. This car was lined with steel to protect the occupants from attacks by angered residents of the community in which the gambling games had been operated. Also the grifters from all circuses associate during the winter season, for many of them spend the winter, or as much of it as their funds permit, in Hot Springs. The grifter in one circus will know the principal grifters in all of the other circuses. This exclusive association is a product of the necessity for training and tutelage in the operation of the gambling games.

Victims are available in practically every community. The general interest in gambling is the basis, but to this are added, first, the general atmosphere of make-believe and celebration connected with the circus, and second, the techniques used in appealing to spectators. One of these techniques is the example of the shill, who appears to be another spectator, but is actually an assistant in the game, and who plays and wins frequently. Another technique is an apparent opportunity for dishonesty; one of the shills raises one of the shells while the operator's back is turned and enables the other spectators to see the pea under the shell, or he bends the corner of the card in the monte game so that the spectator knows which card to guess. Since this dishonesty seems to make the gamble absolutely certain, many spectators then try it, and lose. The suggestions and insistence of the operator and of other assistants who seem to be spectators are factors. Finally, the general method is to induce a spectator to make a start, even without paying, and he is then ashamed to stop after a loss or two.

Dishonest public officials can be found in a large proportion of the communities in which circuses appear. Gambling is at least winked at in most communities, and the officials feel that some gambling in connection with the celebration at the time of a circus can be condoned, especially in return for tickets or money.

Dishonest circus managers are, or at least have been, abundant. The circus thirty years or more ago generally depended on the return from grifting for a substantial part of its income. The circus manager employed a "privilege man" who had charge of all of the grifting, and who paid to the circus a percentage of everything taken in on all of the games. Many of the circus managers started as grifters, and were sympathetic toward the grifters.

These four elements are therefore the necessary characteristics of this behavior system. Circus grifting was authorized and flourished in practically all of the circuses in 1880, in all except Ringlings in 1900, and in all except the largest circuses in 1930. In other words, circus grifting is decreasing. The circus grifters explain that this decrease is not due to a reduction in the number of potential grifters, or in the number of potential victims, or in the number of dishonest public officials. They insist that the decrease is due entirely to the changed attitude of circus managers. Moreover, the changed attitude of the circus manager is not due to an increase in honest motives, but to a change in the economic relationships. In the earlier days the grifting circus could change its name and thus conceal its identity before returning to a community which had been angered by the gambling games on the last trip. As the circus increased in size, its name came to be an asset from the point of view of advertising and could not be changed without loss of prestige and therefore loss of income. The loss from the change of name would be greater than the gain from grifting, and therefore grifting was reluctantly abandoned. It is for that reason that grifting is now found only in the smaller circuses.

The principal question is, Why did the circus ever authorize and participate in grifting? The most immediate answer is that this was a specific manifestation of generally dishonest tendencies. Many circuses in early days were fences for stolen horses. Its employees have been notorious for thefts from clotheslines. The circus management has frequently dealt dishonestly with its employees, holding out a part of the wages, overcharging on expenses. The circus has been unfair in its competition with the other circuses. The men who put up posters in the early decades were necessarily sluggers who could fight with the bill plasterers of rival circuses. Many of the attractions have been frauds. The "garmagunt" with three heads and eight legs was made of sole leather. The Siamese twins were two separate persons with a flesh-colored belt holding them together during the time they were on exhibition. The "horse with its tail where its head ought to be" was discovered, after payment of ten cents, to be a horse with its tail toward the manger. The exhibit "for men only" proved to be a pair of suspenders. The emu eggs sold by the attendant to farmers for $1.50 each proved to be goose eggs. The man who sold balloons hired an assistant to go through the circus grounds and, with his mouth full of tacks, blow them at the balloons which had been purchased so that resales could be made. Hundreds of incidents of this nature are recounted in the histories of the circus.

This general dishonesty, in which the circus grifting was embedded, was a product of four conditions. First, the circus was a mobile organization. It seldom remained longer than one day in a community, and there were no permanent ties, duties, responsibilities, or relationships. The circus was regarded as queer by the community, and the community was regarded as queer by the circus people. Second, the community was hostile toward the circus in several respects. In some places the circus or any other exhibit was prohibited. The opposition was partly on the ground of morals. It was believed that the circus would corrupt the young people. In some communities it was customary for the preachers to agree to preach anti-circus sermons in all churches on the Sunday preceding the circus. To counteract this Barnum advertised moral lectures as a part of the circus program, but the lectures bulked larger in the advertisements than they did in the program. The opposition was also on economic grounds. It was believed that the circus took away from the community money which should be spent in the community. Third, the people of the community frequently were dishonest in their dealings with the circus. The head of the department of streets in one city on the night before the appearance of the circus substituted old, worn-out manhole covers for the ones then in use, so that many of these covers would be broken by the heavy wagons in the circus parade. He then presented to the circus a bill for damages each year until the circus became suspicious and discovered the truth. A woman whose home was adjacent to the circus grounds claimed damages of fifty dollars because her laundry on the clothesline was spotted by flies attracted by the circus. The circus promised to give a free ticket to each child in an orphanage and to enough attendants to take care of the children; when the children arrived each one had an adult attendant. Thus the circus has been confronted with continuous efforts to impose upon it. Fourth, on the basis of this mobility, opposition, and community impositions, the circus population have undoubtedly been selected. It is not a random assortment of the population of the country, but rather is selected for that type of life. They have had a hard, unsociable life, and they have been hard, unsociable people. Out of this has grown the general dishonesty and grifting. It is reported that the English circus, which is much less mobile than the American circus, has very little dishonesty.[3]

CONCLUSION

Professional theft and circus grifting have been described in some detail as illustrations of the point of view and methods which are suggested. Neither of these topics has been investigated exhaustively and the interpretations are therefore tentative and hypothetical. More intensive studies are needed of these two behavior systems and of other behavior systems in crime before general propositions can be developed. . . .

FOOTNOTES

[1]Jerome Hall, *Theft, Law, and Society,* Boston, 1935.

[2]Roger Benton, *Where Do I Go from Here?* New York, 1936; Hutchins Hapgood, *Autobiography of a Thief,* New York, 1903; Will Irwin, *Confessions of a Con Man,* New York, 1909; A. V. Judges, *The Elizabethan Underworld,* London, 1930; John Landesco, "The Criminal Underworld of Chicago in the Eighties and Nineties," *Journal of Criminal Law and Criminology,* (Sept., 1934–March, 1935), 341–357, 928–940; Charles E. Merriam, *Chicago,* New York, 1929, Ch. 2; J. F. Norfleet, *The Amazing Experiences of an Intrepid Texas Rancher,* Rev. Ed., Sugar Land, Tex., 1927; John J. O'Connor, *Broadway Racketeers,* New York, 1928; Edwin H. Sutherland, *The Professional Thief,* Chicago, 1937; Philip S. Van Cise, *Fighting the Underworld,* Boston, 1936.

[3]Bert J. Chipman, *Hey Rube!* Hollywood, 1933; C. R. Cooper, *Circus Day,* New York, 1925; E. C. May, *The Circus from Rome to Ringling,* New York, 1932; Gil Robinson, *Old Wagon Show Days,* Cincinnati, 1925; R. E. Sherwood, *Hold Yer Hosses,* New York, 1932; E. H. Smith, "Grift, An Account Based on Statement by Hoke Hammond," *Collier's,* April 8, 1922, 11–12, 20–21; M. R. Werner, *Barnum,* New York, 1930.

2

BEHAVIOR SYSTEMS AS A FIELD
FOR RESEARCH

A. B. Hollingshead

A large part of the research basic to current sociological theory has been carried on during the last half-century. To be sure, throughout the ages valuable studies have been made occasionally, but never before has there been consistent and continued investigation oriented toward the discovery of the compendent principles of a science of society and culture. Research in sociology, since the World War, has been focused, in the main, on the following fields: (1) social institutions, such as the family and religion; (2) community study and human ecology; (3) social psychology; (4) the processes of culture change; and finally, (5) analysis of the pathological aspects of culture and society. Very few of these investigations have been centered on the many vocations in western civilization. This is an

Reprinted with permission of author and publisher, from *American Sociological Review*, Volume 4, December 1939, pp. 816-822.

ant omission for, as Park has observed, "every occupation mes, or tends to become, the basis for a new society."[1] The esis presented here is that the sociologist and anthropologist should include within the focus of their attention the behavior systems of definable functional groups. This approach entails as a point of departure the definition and characterization of behavior systems.

Persons in more or less continuous association evolve behavior traits and cultural mechanisms which are unique to the group and differ in some way from those of other groups and from the larger socio-cultural complex. That is, every continuing social group develops a variant culture and a body of social relations peculiar and common to its members. This complex on the overt side may be characterized by discernible behavior of the group members in relation to each other, and to those who do not belong; and on the covert side, by an ethos or ideology which includes mores, codes, and other rules, which take the form of sanctions binding upon the membership in their relations to each other and to the external social world.[2] Knowledge, techniques, attitudes, and behavior traits are all integrated into a more or less congruous system within which the participant members orient their lives and acquire status in the community and society. These constitute the criteria by which a specialized group is differentiated from other technical groups, and from the larger, incoherent "Great Society." Such a complex constitutes a behavior system.

The general characteristics of a specific behavior system include the following: (1) a group of specialists recognized by society, as well as by themselves, who possess an identifiable complex of common culture values, communication devices (argot or other symbols), techniques, and appropriate behavior patterns; (2) the acquisition by initiates of the body of esoteric knowledge and appropriate behavior patterns before the novices are accepted by the initiated; (3) appropriate sanctions applied by the membership to control members in their relations with one another and with the larger society, and to control nonmembers in their relations with members. When social relations are confined within the professional sphere, sanctions peculiar to the situation often apply,[3] but when they do not, the sanctions applicable to all members of society are the guides to conduct.

The most ubiquitous behavior systems in our society are integrated around the vocational specialties which characterize and guarantee the ongoing of our technological civilization. This does not mean, however, that behavior systems are limited to vocational groups, for such racial and cultural minorities as the Negroes have a way of life, which might be viewed as a behavior system. Certainly one's vocation determines, in the main, his income, the type of home he lives in, his menu, his associates, and his leisure time activities.[4] A culture complex and a system of social relations associated with it develop around the vocational specialties. This principle is demonstrated in the sociological volumes on specific occupations, such as waitresses in restaurants,[5] salesgirls in department stores,[6] public school teachers,[7] thieves,[8] hoboes,[9] and taxi-dancers.[10] These studies show that the possession of specialized knowledge and techniques combined with behavior peculiar to a vocational group sets its members off from those who belong to another specialized group. These are smaller societies organized within the larger society, related to it in many ways, yet often different in outlook, practices and values. Society, in this sense, may be viewed as a series of general reaction systems integrated around the universals and the basic institutions, and of specific reaction systems associated with the specialized functional groups who possess the esoteric knowledge and techniques necessary for the maintenance of society.

The person is related in many ways to both the general and the specific reactions systems. Generally, the adult specializes in a vocation and thereby identifies himself with a specific group around which his major activities are organized. At the same time, he participates in the general behavior patterns associated with the universals, and incidentally, directly or indirectly, comes in contact with several specific behavior patterns connected with the specialties and the alternatives.[11] These general and specific behavior patterns entailed in the person's participation in culture control his behavior under almost all circumstances in relation to the common institutions, to particular persons, and to groups which come within the interactional horizon[12] of the person's activities in society. In this sense, there are two varieties of socio-cultural behavior systems: the general, correlated with the cultural universals; and the specific, associated with the specialties. Sumner recognized the existence of both varieties and suggested that the subject matter of sociology might be composed of knowledge derived from their study.[13]

Analysis of behavior systems should be concentrated on three problems: the definition of the system; its life history; and its relation to the larger society.

Definition means not only the discovery of the concatenation of techniques and traits associated with the system, but also the delimitation of the complex from other social systems, and from the larger society. To do this, a constant search for the characteristics peculiar to the system must be uppermost in the student's program; a search for the specific elements is implied here, which integrate the connected techniques, values, and behavior patterns of the person in his relations with the group, of other members with him, and their interactions with society, and vice versa. In the study of specific behavior systems, the sociologist should not be concerned with the technical aspects of a particular speciality *per se,* but he must take into consideration how these techniques are acquired and how they operate in conditioning the interactional pattern of the person in his relations to others within the group and those who belong to other systems. The analysis of society and culture within the frame of reference of behavior systems will reveal many types, ranging from the altruistic complex associated with social work to the predatory activities of the professional criminal, racketeer, prostitute, and corrupt politician. Within the gamut listed above, lie all the socially useful and necessary specialities connected with the day-to-day functioning of a community and society.

The second phase of the problem is oriented around the question as to how a system comes into existence, is maintained from generation to generation, and perhaps passes away. The conditions inherent in the general culture that give rise to new behavior systems, and the dissolution of long established ones are a vital part of the dynamics of culture. Behavior systems probably evolve in a manner similar to other phases of culture, but the process needs to be studied carefully before theoretically valid statements can be formulated. Tentatively, it is safe to hypothecate that a specific system changes through the invention of new techniques, the discovery of new knowledge, the adoption and assimilation of traits evolved by other groups. Since social action patterns are passed from one generation to another, frequently with only superficial modifications, the transmission process is an integral part of a system's life history. Transmission is focused on the initiate who must shape his behavior according to values, codes, techniques, and group expectancies, if he is to be accepted as a member of the system, and therefore as a colleague. By conformity to the behavior system, the initiate acquires a status within the group and a position within the community. Transmission of the system from the initiated to the novice is a groupwise process participated in by all members of the specialty in association with the initiate. It is also aided by members of the larger society who accord to the initiate appropriate deference, and behave toward him in the socially prescribed ways. Just what these ways are needs to be studied. The transmission process has two actional phases, the one just mentioned, namely, from the group's viewpoint; the other, from the viewpoint of the person. How the novice assimilates, and becomes a part of the system is of crucial importance. Once the novitiate is over and the person is accepted by his associates as within the system, he is in a position to help in its maintenance and transmission, because the behavior of a person in a specific system is not unique to that person but is common to all who belong to the system and participate in it. It is assumed a person adjusted to the particular system which integrates his major social function is generally satisfied with his way of life and orients his activities toward achieving success as it is defined by the social values inherent in the system. This assumption brings to the fore a pertinent question: What value does the system have for the participant members; or, how does the system satisfy the person who follows it?

The third problem is the relation of the specific system, and the persons who function within it, to the larger society. As pointed out above, the concatenation of culture complex and correlated behavior patterns fuse in the thoughts and actions of the participants in a configuration, and thereby create and maintain a behavior system. Insofar as the group's culture is unique, it is differentiated, therefore, from the larger social organization attributed to society. Some relevant questions to be kept in mind then are: What is the role a given system plays in social organization or disorganization? how does it influence the development of personality? does it foster cooperative social relationships? Finally, what other elements and ideas are inherent in the system which will add to sociological knowledge of the relations between society and its component parts?

There are two objectives of research hypothecated in this paper. The first objective is a detailed study of specific systems directed toward *the formulation of general propositions indispensable to sociological theory about behavior systems.* It is assumed that such analysis will yield knowledge on the processes inherent in the complexes which organize and disorganize persons and groups, as well as on culture and society. The second objective is the discovery of *the relation of the behavior system to the person in his interactional group.* Incidentally, this variety of research is concerned with finding how the values of a functional group influence a member's conduct in relation to his fellows, to the larger society, as well as the reaction these cohesive group mores have on the mores common to society. The detailed relationships, techniques, values, and traits which circumscribe and compose specific behavior systems will have to be revealed by research. Once this knowledge has been accumulated, man may be able intelligently to control social processes associated with behavior systems in relation to general society.

The points outlined in the preceding paragraphs may be illustrated briefly by sketching some of the characteristics inherent in the behavior system of professional cooks.[14] The personnel of the profession is drawn from various nationality groups and cultural enclaves, but they have been moulded into cooks by common experiences. The social function around which their activities are integrated is the preparation of food for the general public in hotels and restaurants. Both society and the members of the profession recognize the existence of the vocation and its importance. Cooks believe their profession is just as vital in the social scheme as law, medicine, teaching, or any other specialized activity. A common belief among them is the following: "If people would eat right, and food was cooked right, doctors would starve to death." There is also a feeling that a cook can go just as far in his profession as he desires: "The chef in the Drake hotel makes as much as the president of the

United States." The possession of common knowledge, techniques, and values means that one cook can recognize another cook when they meet professionally; furthermore, each can readily determine what kind of a cook the other is. For instance, "You can't lie about where you have worked, and what you have done, because a chef in a first class place knows how things are done in other first class places."

Future cooks are selected from among the present dishwashers: "cooks start out by washing dishes." The more ambitious and intelligent dishwashers soon work into the menial jobs around the kitchen. They gradually learn how to do the different specialized jobs such as salads, desserts, roasts, broiling, soups, and so on. Cooks, on the whole are very mobile for two reasons. First, "the way to learn to cook is to work only in first class places, and move as soon as you have learned all you can in one place." A successful chef specializes in many branches of cookery, and the way to learn the art of blending ingredients is to work with men noted in the profession for special dishes. To do this, the apprentice cook must travel to these men and learn from them. This may involve traveling to every important city in the nation, and possibly Europe, to gain this training. The second reason cooks move is the nature of the recreational season in the United States. Practically all hotels, no matter whether they are located in cities or resort areas, have a definite season. During the season, the demand for skilled help is great, but with the end of the season the hotel may close, or keep only a skeleton crew. For instance, Florida and California have winter seasons, New England and the Great Lakes region, summer seasons; Atlantic City and the Gulf Coast are again summer areas. The seasonal nature of employment forces cooks to migrate from one area to another; south in the winter, or to the cities, and north again in the summer. Not only are there peak loads during the year, but also during the day. The cook's daily activities are centered around preparing highly different groups of foods for the three meals. Since his work is concentrated into three rush hours, the ruling code in the kitchen and dining room is cooperation between dishwashers, bus boys, waiters, and cooks. Cooperation is necessary because meals have to be served in a hurry to hungry patrons. Any balking on the job, or failure to dovetail into the organization, means dismissal. "The cook who won't cooperate lasts only one day."

Leisure time activities are concentrated around drinking, gambling, dancing, and shows. Playing the races in the winter, and attending baseball games in the summer are their chief diversions. These activities are carried on in their common hangouts, third class hotels, taverns, and poolhalls. Every city has its "spots" where kitchen help congregate. Although drinking is prevalent among cooks, they are very seldom jailed because the police know them, and are almost friendly. "A cop will take a drunken cook home and put him to bed, and the next day the cook will feed the cop." Practically all cooks are men, and most of them are single. In their relations with women, they generally go out with waitresses, or visit prostitutes. When they marry and settle down the girl is usually an ex-waitress. Many cooks save money and open up a business of their own; this applies especially to Germans, Greeks, and Italians, but less generally to Americans. The behavior system peculiar to cooks needs to be studied systematically before any of the data sketched here can be organized into a body of correlated propositions. The purpose of giving this material has been to indicate the nature of the things the student may find when he goes to work.

Those who are already interested in the study of behavior systems are aware of the wealth of available material. In every community, there are many specialized occupations, each a veritable mine. Urban communities are particularly useful for the type of analysis proposed here, because of the many differentiations which characterize the behavior of their inhabitants. What is particularly appealing about this form of research is the fact that sociologists in small colleges may study, without great expense, the types about them. The field for study is limited only by the number of identifiable variant cultures and correlated behavior systems. For instance, there are many action systems in the field of crime such as professional theft, gambling, racketeering, robbery, blackmail, political graft, corruption, and so on. Actors, professional writers, lumberjacks, waiters, policemen, undertakers, junkmen, sailors, railway specialists[15] such as engineers, firemen, conductors, brakemen, telegraphers, and section workers, only to mention a few types, are all illustrations of the raw materials to which the student of society may profitably turn his hand.

Those in especially favorable areas, such as around Los Angeles, might well study the variant cultures and correlated behavior systems connected with the motion picture industry's personnel. Certainly this highly selected group has a way of life far different from the farmer, doctor, or stone mason. In the South, there are many sources of raw material such as the Negro doctor, lawyer, yard-boy, cotton farmer; equally as interesting to study would be the poor white sharecropper, or the aristocratic planter. Those in seacoast cities might study well-known types connected with the sea.

By way of summary we may point out that, until a considerable number of these actions systems have been studied, the sociologist's knowledge of the reciprocal nature of culture, society, and the person perforce must remain vague and at best highly fragmentary. A science of society must be derived from a knowledge of society and the only way to gain such knowledge is to study the person in relation to other persons and groups as they function within the milieu of their specific participation in culture and society. Finally, the purpose of this paper is to call attention to the possibilities of behavior system analysis, and perhaps stimulate research along the line indicated in the preceding paragraphs.

FOOTNOTES

[1]R. E. Park, in the Introduction to F. R. Donovan, *The Saleslady*, vii, Chicago, 1930.

[2]For realistic description of this process, as well as an analysis of a behavior system, see E. H. Sutherland, *The Professional Thief*, Chicago, 1937, 3–26.

[3]*Ibid.*, various sections, but especially 82–139.

[4]See R. S. and H. M. Lynd, *Middletown*, New York, 1929, 53–89. Also, *Middletown in Transition*, New York, 1937, 7–73.

[5]F. R. Donovan, *The Woman Who Waits*, Chicago, 1920.

[6]F. R. Donovan, *The Saleslady*, Chicago, 1931.

[7]F. R. Donovan, *The Schoolma'am*, New York, 1938.

[8]E. H. Sutherland, *The Professional Thief*, Chicago, 1937.

[9]Nels Anderson, *The Hobo*, Chicago, 1923.

[10]Paul G. Cressey, *The Taxi-Dance Hall*, Chicago, 1932, especially 31–108.

[11]For a discussion of these terms see Ralph Linton, *The Study of Man*, New York, 1936, 272–274.

[12]Edward Sapir, "The Emergence of the Concept of Personality in a Study of Culture," *Journal of Social Psychology* (1935), 408–415.

[13] W. G. Sumner, *Folkways,* Boston, 1906, 34, 39.

[14]The information given here has been collected from professional cooks in a casual manner as a preliminary phase of a more intensive study. The statements of the cooks represent the ideologies of cooks rather than verified facts.

[15]See W. F. Cottrell, "Of Time and the Railroader," *American Sociological Review* (April, 1939), 190–198, for a description of the influence of time in the railroader's life organization.

3

THE CONCEPT OF THE SUB-CULTURE
AND ITS APPLICATION

Milton M. Gordon

One of the functions of any science, "natural" or "social," is admittedly to discover and isolate increasingly smaller units of its subject matter. This process leads to more extensive control of variables in experiment and analysis. There are times, however, when the scientist must put some of these blocks back together again in an integrated pattern. This is especially true where the patterning reveals itself as a logical necessity, with intrinsic connections which create something more, so to speak, than the mere sum of the parts. Specifically, in the social sciences, this patterning is necessary where the impact of the nexus on the human being is that of a unit, and not a series of disconnected social situations. This paper represents an

Reprinted with permission of author and publisher from *Social Forces*, Volume 26, October 1947, pp. 40-42.

to delineate such a nexus by a logical extension of the
t of culture.

merican sociologists, on the whole, have seemed reluctant to
ext...d the concept of culture beyond the point where it has already
been developed and more or less handed to us by the anthropologists.
We hear an occasional reference to "urban culture," or "rural
culture," or "the culture of the middle class," but these references
have seemed to represent sporadic resting-places of semantic convenience rather than any systematic application of the term to
well-defined social situations. Broadly speaking, we have been content
to stop the concept of culture at national boundaries, and engage in
our intra-national analyses in terms of the discrete units of ethnic
background, social class, regional residence, religious affiliation, and
so on. It is the thesis of this paper that a great deal could be gained
by a more extensive use of the concept of the *sub-culture*—a concept
used here to refer to a sub-division of a national culture, composed
of a combination of factorable social situations such as class status,
ethnic background, regional and rural or urban residence, and
religious affiliation, but *forming in their combination a functioning
unity which has an integrated impact on the participating individual.*
No claim is made here for origination of the term. Although its use
has apparently not been extensive enough to merit it a place in the
Dictionary of Sociology, edited by Fairchild,[1] a recent and perceptive
use of the term has been made in a paper by Green, where he speaks
incidentally of "highly organized subcultures," and, in connection
with the question of neuroses, phrases a query in the following
manner: "Since in modern society no individual participates in the
total cultural complex totally but primarily in a series of population
segments grouped according to sex, age, class, occupation, region,
religion, and ethnic group—all with somewhat differing norms and
expectations of conduct—how do these combine in different ways to
form varying backgrounds for individual etiologies of neurotic
trends?"[2]

Green, by implication, uses the terms "sub-culture" and "population segment" interchangeably. Nomenclature is relatively unimpor-
tant so long as it is consistent, but we prefer the former term since it
seems to emphasize more directly the dynamic character of the

framework within which the child is socialized. It is a world within a world, so to speak, but it *is* a world. The emphasis in this paper, then, is simply on the unifying and transmuting implications of the term "sub-culture" for such combinations of factors as ethnic group, social class, region, occupation, religion, and urban or rural residence, and on the need for its wider application.

A primary and major implication of this position is that the child growing up in a particular sub-culture feels its impact as a unit. For instance, the son of lower-class Italian immigrants, growing up in New York's upper East Side, is not a person who is simultaneously affected by separable items consisting of ethnic background, low-economic status, and a highly urbanized residential situation. He is a person whose environmental background is an interwoven and variegated combination of all these factors. Each of the elements has been somewhat transformed by virtue of its combination with the others. This fact must be taken into consideration in research procedures dealing with environmental backgrounds and their effects. A corollary of this position is that identically named factors in different sub-cultures are not interchangeable. Thus being a middle-class Jew is not the same thing as being a middle-class Gentile except for the additional factor of being Jewish.

A wider use of the concept of the *sub-culture* would, in the opinion of this writer, give us a keen and incisive tool which would, on the one hand, prevent us from making too broad groupings where such inclusiveness is not warranted (we would, for instance, refer not so much to "the Negro," as to "Southern, rural, lower-class Negroes," or "North, urban, middle-class Negroes," etc.[3]), and, on the other hand, enable us to discern relatively closed and cohesive systems of social organization which currently we tend to analyze separately with our more conventional tools of "class" and "ethnic group." The writer, for instance, has been interested to observe in the city of Philadelphia a not entirely cohesive, but unmistakably present, sub-culture composed of members of the Society of Friends (Quakers), and ranging in class position from upper-middle to upper-upper. More conventional objects of sociological attention, second and third generation Jews, would seem, for the most part, to be neither "marginal men" in the Park and Stonequist phrase, nor competitors in the social class system with white Gentiles, but rather members of highly integrated "marginal sub-cultures" (called marginal here because, like the "marginal man," these sub-cultures composed of the descendants of immigrant Jews lie somewhere between the immigrant culture and the native Gentile culture and contain cultural contributions from both) whose variable elements are size of community of residence and social class.

A distinction must, of course, be made between separate sub-cultures and separate units of the same sub-culture. Thus lower-class white Protestants in one medium-sized New England city would presumably belong to the same sub-culture as lower-class white Protestants in another medium-sized New England community hundreds of miles away, though each group would constitute a separate unit. Whether lower-class white Protestants in a medium-sized community in the Middle-West would form a different sub-culture is a more difficult point. The question of whether variation of one factor is sufficient to set up a separate sub-culture would have to be answered empirically by a field study of the community situations in question.

A comprehensive application of the sub-cultural concept to the American scene would, in time, lead to the delineation of a fairly large number of sub-cultures of varying degrees of cohesiveness and with varying patterns of interaction with each other. Among the many further research problems which such an analysis would pose, six of particular interest to the writer are mentioned here:

1. How do the various sub-cultures rank on a scale of differential access to the rewards of the broader American culture, including both material rewards and status?

2. How is the experience of growing up in a particular sub-culture reflected in the personality structure of the individual? Is there a portion of the personality which is roughly equivalent to a similar portion of the personality of every other individual who has matured in the same sub-culture, and which might, then, be referred to as the "sub-cultural personality"? If Kardiner's hypothesis of a common "basic personality structure" for all participants in the same national culture[4] is valid, it would seem equally likely that a second tier of the personality, so to speak, would consist of the "sub-cultural personality structure."

3. In what way are identical elements of the national culture refracted differentially in the sub-culture? We have been prone, perhaps, to assume uniformities which do not entirely exist. Football, to male adolescents of one sub-culture may mean the chance to hawk programs and peanuts and make some money, to those of another, enthusiastic attendance at the High School game on Saturday afternoon, and to those of still a third, inviting girls up to the campus for a houseparty week-end.

4. What are the most indicative indices of participation in a particular sub-culture? If any one had to be singled out, the writer would offer speech patterns (particularly pronunciation and inflection) as at once the easiest to "observe" and the most revealing. Clothes would probably rank next in indicativeness and ease of discernability—contrary to casual opinion, for men as well as women.

5. What explains the "deviant," that is, the person who does not develop the sub-cultural or social personality characteristic of the particular sub-culture in which he was born and nurtured? An interesting question here is whether there are particular combinations of biological characteristics which would adjust more or less easily to the sub-cultural personalities specifically demanded. What about the above-average in intelligence and sensitive boy, for instance, born into a sub-culture of low-status and rather rough behavior patterns? or, conversely, the son of professional parents who cannot make the grade at college but would much rather be out tinkering with the motor of his automobile?

6. In upward social mobility, does a change of "sub-cultural personality" invariably accompany acquisition of some of the more objective indices of higher status, such as wealth or more highly valued occupation? If not, what stresses and strains result? This last question, in the writer's opinion, is a most interesting one, and in the growing literature on social mobility, to his knowledge, has barely been touched.

FOOTNOTES

[1]Henry Pratt Fairchild, ed., *Dictionary of Sociology,* New York, 1944; the nearest concept in the *Dictionary* is that of the "culture-sub-area," which is defined as "a sub-division of a larger culture area, distinguished by the

comparative completeness of the development of a particular culture trait, or the comparative readiness with which such a trait will be diffused" (p. 83). The emphasis here is obviously on *area*—physical contiguity, which factor may, or may not, or may only partially be present in the *sub-culture*. Thus groups of lower-class white Protestants may live in different sections of the same city. Or middle-class Jews may be scattered over a medium-sized city and still form a social entity (see, for instance, W. Lloyd Warner and Leo Srole, *The Social Systems of American Ethnic Groups,* Yankee City Series, Vol. 3, New Haven: 1945, 51).

[2]Arnold W. Green, "Sociological Analysis of Horney and Fromm," *The American Journal of Sociology* (May 1946), 534.

[3]The writer is aware of the increasing attention which is being given, especially to class-differentiation in the Negro group. Progress in this direction with other ethnic groups, such as, for instance, the Jews, has not been so marked.

[4]Abram Kardiner, *The Individual and His Society,* New York, 1939. See particularly p. vi, and p. 12.

Part Two

SUBCULTURE
BOUNDARIES

Sociologists, like all other members of society, tend to reify their concepts. Once we decide that imposing the concept "subculture" on reality helps us to understand that reality, we risk forgetting that the concept began as an artificial construct. Too often we treat subcultures as though each was surrounded by a twelve-foot high barbed-wire fence. For a few subcultures, perhaps the Amish or the Gypsies, this does not do great violence to the data—yet even where there is a literal fence, as in prisons, subculture boundaries are often diffuse, as Irwin and Cressey demonstrate in Chapter Six.

For most subcultures the exact boundaries are impossible to locate with any precision, and thus the fact that we are working with abstractions must not be forgotten. Yablonsky's discussion of "near-groups" in Chapter Four offers one formulation for remembering this. The writer's focus is delinquency, but—as with the other essays concerned with crime or delinquency in this book—the formulations are easily generalized to broader subcultural concerns. In Chapter Five Miller argues that the delinquent subculture cannot be viewed in isolation. Rather, he says, its boundaries overlap those of the lower class subculture, and thus to comprehend gang delinquency we must examine lower-class subculture and the boundary relations between the two.

In Chapter Six Irwin and Cressey present a further example of the interpenetration of subcultures. Of particular interest are their comments on page 78, concerning the problem of perceiving the differences between subcultures and the blending of subcultures that occurs in some situations. Finally, in Chapter Seven, I attempt to pull together these and some other threads, to spell out various aspects of the issue of subculture boundaries, and to develop a notion of subculture marginality that can cope with these issues.

4

THE DELINQUENT GANG
AS A NEAR-GROUP

Lewis Yablonsky

This paper is based on four years of research and direct work with some thirty delinquent gangs in New York City. . . .

Although data were obtained on 30 gangs, the study focused on two, the Balkans and the Egyptian Kings. It was the latter which committed the brutal killing of a polio victim, Michael Farmer, in an upper West Side park of New York City. The trial lasted over three months and received nation-wide attention. These two groups were intensively interviewed and contributed heavily to the formulation of a theory of near-groups. In addition to the analysis of the gang's structure, a number of delinquent gang war events produced vital case material.

There is a paucity of available theory based on empirical

Reprinted with permission of the author and The Society for the Study of Social Problems, from *Social Problems*, Volume 7, Fall 1959, pp. 108-117.

evidence about the structure of delinquent gangs. Two landmarks in the field are Thrasher's *The Gang* and Whyte's *Street Corner Society*. Some recent publications and controversy focus on the emergence of gangs and their function for gang members. Professor Cohen deals with gangs as sub-cultures organized by working-class boys as a reaction to middle-class values.[1] In a recent publication Block and Nederhoffer discuss gangs as organizations designed to satisfy the adolescent's striving for the attainment of adult status.[2]

Although partial group structuring has been extensively discussed in sociological literature on "groups," "crowds," and "mobs," my gang research revealed that these collectivity constructs did not seem to adequately describe and properly abstract the underlying structural characteristics of the delinquent gang. Consequently, I have attempted here to construct a formulation which would draw together various described social dimensions of the gang under one conceptual scheme. I call this formulation Near-Group Theory.

NEAR-GROUP THEORY

One way of viewing human collectivities is on a continuum of organization characteristics. At one extreme, we have a highly organized, cohesive, functioning collection of individuals as members of a sociological group. At the other extreme, we have a mob of individuals characterized by anonymity, disturbed leadership, motivated by emotion, and in some cases representing a destructive collectivity within the inclusive social system. When these structures are observed in extreme, their form is apparent to the observer. However, in viewing these social structures on a continuum, those formations which tend to be neither quite a cohesive integrated group nor a disturbed mal-functioning mob or crowd are often distorted by observers in one or the other direction.

A central thesis of this paper is that mid-way on the group-mob continuum are collectivities which are neither groups nor mobs. These are structures prevalent enough in a social system to command attention in their own right as constructs for sociological analysis. Near-groups are characterized by some of the following factors: (1)

diffuse role definition, (2) limited cohesion, (3) impermanence, (4) minimal consensus of norms, (5) shifting membership, (6) disturbed leadership, and (7) limited definition of membership expectations. These factors characterize the near-group's "normal" structure.

True groups may manifest near-group structure under stress, in transition, or when temporarily disorganized; however, at these times they are moving toward or away from their normative, permanent structure. The near-group manifests its homeostasis in accord with the factors indicated. It never fully becomes a *group* or a *mob*.

THE GANG AS A NEAR-GROUP PATTERN

Some recent sociological theory and discourse on gangs suffers from distortions of gang structure to fit a group rather than a near-group conception. Most gang theorizing begins with an automatic assumption that gangs are defined sociological groups. Many of these misconceived theories about gangs in sociological treatises are derived from the popular and traditional image of gangs held by the general public as reported in the press, rather than as based upon empirical scientific investigation. The following case material reveals the disparities between popular reports of gang war behavior and their organization as revealed by more systematic study.

The official report of a gang fight, which made headlines in New York papers as the biggest in the city's history, detailed a gang war between six gangs over a territorial dispute.[3] The police, social workers, the press, and the public accepted a defined version of groups meeting in battle over territory. Research into this gang war incident, utilizing a near-group concept of gangs, indicates another picture of the situation. . . .

Depth interviews with 40 gang boys, most of whom had been arrested at the scene of the gang fight, revealed a variety of reasons for attendance at the battle. There were also varied perceptions of the event and the gangs involved reported simply in the press as "gangs battling over territory." . . .

Estimates of number of gang boys present varied from 80 to 5,000.

Gang boys interviewed explained their presence at the "battle" as follows:

I didn't have anything to do that night and wanted to see what was going to happen.

Those guys called me a Spic and I was going to get even. [He made this comment even though the "rival" gangs were mostly Puerto Ricans.] . . .

I always like a fight; it keeps up my rep.

My father threw me out of the house; I wanted to get somebody and heard about the fight.

The youth who was responsible for "calling on" the gang war—the reputed Balkan Gang leader—presented this version of the event:

That night I was out walkin' my dog about 7:30. Then I saw all these guys coming from different directions. I couldn't figure out what was happening. Then I saw some of the guys I know and I remembered we had called it on for that night.

I never really figured the Politicians [a supposed "brother Gang" he had called] would show.

Another boy added another dimension to "gang war organization":

How did we get our name? Well, when we were in the police station, the cops kept askin' us who we were. Jay was studying history in school—so he said how about The Balkans. Let's call ourselves Balkans. So we told the cops—we're the Balkans—and that was it.

Extensive data revealed this was not a case of two organized groups meeting in battle. The press, public, police, social workers, and others projected group conceptions onto a near-group activity. Most of the youths at the scene of the gang war were, in fact, participating in a kind of mob action. Most had no real concept of belonging to any gang or group; however, they were interested in a situation which might be exciting and possibly a channel for expressing some of their aggressions and hostilities. Although it was not necessarily a defined war, the possibilities of a stabbing or even a killing were high—with a few hundred disturbed and fearful youths milling around in the undefined situation. The gang war was not a social situation of two structured teen-aged armies meeting on a battlefield to act out a defined situation; it was a case of two near-groups in action.

Another boy's participation in this gang war further reveals its structure. The evening of the fight he had nothing to do, heard about this event and decided that he would wander up to see what was going to happen. On his way to the scene of the rumored gang fight he thought it might be a good idea to invite a few friends "just to be on the safe side." This swelled the final number of youths arriving at the scene of the gang fight, since other boys did the same. He denied (and I had no reason to disbelieve him) belonging to either of the gangs and the same applied to his friends. He was arrested at the scene of "battle" for disorderly conduct and weapon-carrying.

I asked him why he had carried a knife and a zip gun on his person when he went to the gang fight if he did not belong to either of the reputed gangs and intended to be merely a "peaceful observer." His response: "Man, I'm not going to a rumble without packin'." The boy took along weapons for self-defense in the event he was attacked. The possibilities of his being attacked in an hysterical situation involving hundreds of youths who had no clear idea of what they were doing at the scene of a gang fight was, of course, great. Therefore, he was correct (within his social framework) in taking along a weapon for self-protection.

These characteristic responses to the situation when multiplied by the numbers of others present characterizes the problem. What may be a confused situation involving many aggressive youths (belonging to near-groups) is often defined as a case of two highly mechanized and organized gang groups battling each other with definition to their activities.

In another "gang war case" which made headlines, a psychotic youth acted out his syndrome by stabbing another youth. When arrested and questioned about committing the offense, the youth stated that he was a member of a gang carrying out retaliation against another gang, which was out to get him. He attributed his assault to gang affiliation.

The psychotic youth used the malleable near-group, the gang, *as his psychotic* syndrome. Napoleon, God, Christ, and other psychotic syndromes, so popular over the years, may have been replaced on city streets by gang membership. Not only is it a convenient syndrome, but some disturbed youths find their behavior as rational, accepted, and even aggrandized by many representatives of society. Officials such as police officers and social workers, in their interpretation of the incident, often amplify this individual behavior by a youth into a group gang war condition because it is a seemingly more logical explanation of a senseless act.

In the case of the Balkans, the societal response of viewing them as a group rather than a near-group solidified their structure. After the incident, as one leader stated it, "lots more kids wanted to join."

Another gang war event further reveals the near-group structure of the gang. On the night of July 30, 1957, a polio victim named Michael Farmer was beaten and stabbed to death by a gang varyingly known as the Egyptian Kings and the Dragons. The boys who participated in this homicide came from the upper West Side of Manhattan. I had contact with many of these boys prior to the event and was known to others through the community program I directed. Because of this prior relationship the boys cooperated and responded openly when I interviewed them in the institutions where they were being held in custody.

Responses to my interviews indicated the near-group nature of the gang. Some of the pertinent responses which reveal this characteristic of the Egyptian King gang structure are somewhat demonstrated by the following comments made by [three] of the participants in the killing. (These are representative comments selected from over ten hours of recorded interviews.)

> *I was walking uptown with a couple of friends and we ran into Magician [one of the Egyptian King gang leaders] and them there. They asked us if we wanted to go to a fight, and we said yes. When he asked me if I wanted to go to a fight, I couldn't say no. I mean, I could say no, but for old time's sake, I said yes. . . .*
> *They have guys watching you and if you don't stab or hit*

somebody, they get you later. I hit him over the head with a bat. [Gang youths are unable to articulate specific individuals of the vague "they" who watch over them.]

I don't know how many guys are in the gang. They tell me maybe a hundred or a thousand. I don't know them all. [Each boy interviewed had a different image of the gang.]

These comments and others revealed the gang youths' somewhat different perceptions and rationale of gang war activity. There is a limited consensus of participants as to the nature of gang war situations because the gang structure—the collectivity which defines gang war behavior—is amorphous, diffuse, and malleable.

Despite the fact of gang phenomena taking a diffuse form, theoreticians, social workers, the police, the press, and the public autistically distort gangs and gang behavior toward a gestalt of clarity. The rigid frame of perceiving gangs as groups should shift to the fact of gangs as near-groups. This basic redefinition is necessary if progress is to be made in sociological diagnosis as a foundation for delinquent gang prevention and correction.

THE DETACHED GANG WORKER

The detached-worker approach to dealing with gangs on the action level is increasingly employed in large cities and urban areas throughout the country. Simply stated, a professional, usually a social worker, contacts a gang in their milieu on the street corner and attempts to redirect their delinquent patterns into constructive behavior.

Because of the absence of an adequate perceptual framework, such as the near-group concept, detached gang workers deal with gang collectivities as if they were organized like other groups and social organizations. The following principle stated in a New York City Youth Board manual on the detached gang worker approach reveals this point of view:

Participation in a street gang or club, like participation in any natural group, is a part of the growing-up process of adolescence. Such primary group associations possess potentialities for positive growth and development. Through such a group, the individual can gain security and develop positive ways of living with other individuals. Within the structure of his group the individual can develop such characteristics as loyalty, leadership, and community responsibility.[4]

This basic misconception not only produces inaccurate reports and theories about gang structure but causes ineffectual work with gangs on the action level. This problem of projecting group structure onto gangs may be further illuminated by a cursory examination of detached gang-worker projects.

Approaching the gang as a group, when it is not, tends to project onto it a structure which formerly did not exist. The gang worker's usual set of notions about gangs as groups includes some of the following distortions: (1) the gang has a measurable number of members, (2) membership is defined, (3) the role of members is specified, (4) there is a consensus of understood gang norms among gang members, and (5) gang leadership is clear and entails a flow of authority and direction of action.

These expectations often result in a group-fulfilling prophecy. A group may form as a consequence of the gang worker's view. In one case a gang worker approached two reputed gang leaders and told them he would have a bus to take their gang on a trip to the country. This gang had limited organization; however, by travel-time there were 32 gang members ready to go on the trip. The near-group became more organized as a result of the gang worker's misconception.

This gang from a near-group point of view was in reality comprised of a few disturbed youths with rich delusional systems who had need to view themselves as leaders controlling hordes of other gang boys in their fantasy. Other youths reinforce this ill-defined collectivity for a variety of personal reasons and needs. The gang, in fact, had a shifting membership, no clarity as to what membership entailed, and individualized member images of gang size and function.

The detached worker, as an agent of the formal social system, may thus move in on a gang and give a formerly amorphous collectivity structure and purpose through the projection of group structure onto a near-group.

NEAR-GROUP STRUCTURE

Research into the structure of 30 groups revealed three characteristic levels of membership organization. In the center of the gang, on the first level, are the most psychologically disturbed members—the leaders. It is these youths who require and need the gang most of all. This core of disturbed youths provides the gang's most cohesive force. In a gang of some 30 boys there may be five or six who are central or core members because they desperately need the gang in order to deal with their personal problems of inadequacy. These are youths always working to keep the gang together and in action, always drafting, plotting, and talking gang warfare. They are the center of the near-group activity.

At a second level of near-group organization in the gang, we have youths who claim affiliation to the gang but only participate in it according to their emotional needs at given times. For example, one of the Egyptian Kings reported that if his father had not given him a "bad time" and kicked him out of the house the night of the homicide, he would not have gone to the corner and become involved in the Michael Farmer killing. This second-level gang member's participation in the gang killing was a function of his disturbance on that particular evening. This temporal gang need is a usual occurrence.

At a third level of gang participation, we have peripheral members who will join in with gang activity on occasion, although they seldom identify themselves as members of the gang at times. This type of gang member is illustrated by the youth who went along with the Egyptian Kings on the night of the Farmer killing, as he put it, "for old time's sake." He just happened to be around on that particular evening and went along due to a situational condition. He never really "belonged" to the gang nor was he defined by himself or others as a gang member.

The size of gangs is determined in great measure by the emotional needs of its members at any given point. It is not a measure of actual and live membership. Many of the members exist only on the thought level. In the gang, if the boys feel particularly hemmed in (for paranoid reasons), they will expand the number of their near-group. On the other hand, at other times when they feel secure, the gang's size is reduced to include only those youths known on a face-to-face basis. The research revealed that, unlike an actual group, no member of a near-group can accurately determine the number of its membership at a particular point in time.

For example, most any university department member will tell you the number of other individuals who comprise the faculty of their department. It is apparent that if there are eight members in a department of psychology, each member will know each other member, his role, and the total number of members of the department. In contrast, in examining the size of gangs or near-group participation, the size increases in almost direct relationship to the lack of membership clarity. That is, the second- and third-level members are modified numerically with greater ease than the central members. Third level members are distorted at times to an almost infinite number.

In one interview, a gang leader distorted the size and affiliations of the gang as his emotional state shifted. In an hour interview, the size of his gang varied from 100 members to 4,000, from five brother gangs or alliances to 60, from about ten square blocks of territorial control to include jurisdiction over the five boroughs of New York City, New Jersey, and part of Philadelphia.

Another characteristic of the gang is its lack of role definition. Gang boys exhibit considerable difficulty and contradiction in their roles in the gang. They may say that the gang is organized for protection and that one role of a gang is to fight. How, when, whom, and for what reason he is to fight are seldom clear. The right duties and obligations associated with the gang member's role in the gang varies from gang boy to gang boy.

One gang boy may define himself as a protector of the younger boys in the neighborhood. Another defines his role in the gang as "We are going to get all those guys who call us Spics." Still other gang boys define their participation in the gang as involuntarily forced upon them, through their being "drafted." Moreover, few gang members maintain a consistent function or role within the gang organization.

Definition of membership is vague and indefinite. A youth will say he belongs one day and will quit the next without necessarily telling any other gang member. I would ask one gang boy who came into my office daily whether he was a Balkan. This was comparable to asking him, "How do you feel today?"

Because of limited social ability to assume rights, duties, and obligations in constructive solidified groups, the gang boy attaches himself to a structure which requires limited social ability and can itself be modified to fit his monetary needs. This malleability factor is characteristic of the near-group membership. As roles are building blocks of a group, diffuse role definitions fit in adequately to the near-group which itself has diverse and diffuse objectives and goals. The near-group, unlike a true group, has norms, roles, functions, cohesion, size, and goals which are shaped by the emotional needs of its members.

GANG LEADERSHIP CHARACTERISTICS

Another aspect of near-groups is the factor of self-appointed leadership, usually of a dictatorial, authoritarian type. In interviewing hundreds of gang members one finds that many of them give themselves some role of leadership. For example, in the Egyptian Kings, approximately five boys defined themselves as "war counsellors." It is equally apparent that, except on specific occasions, no one will argue with this self-defined role. Consequently, leadership in the gang may be assumed by practically any member of the gang if he so determines and emotionally needs the power of being a leader at the time. It is not necessary to have his leadership role ratified by his constituents.

Another aspect of leadership in the gang is the procedure of "drafting" or enlisting new members. In many instances, this pattern of coercion to get another youth to join or belong to the gang becomes an end in itself, rather than a means to an end. In short, the process of inducing, coercing, and threatening violence upon another youth, under the guise of getting him to join, is an important gang leader activity. The gang boy is not truly concerned with acquiring another gang member, since the meaning of membership is vague at best; however, acting the power role of a leader forcing another youth to do something against his will becomes meaningful to the "drafter."

GANG FUNCTIONS

In most groups some function is performed or believed to be performed. The function which it performs may be a constructive one, as in an industrial organization, a P.T.A. group, or a political party. On the other hand, it may be a socially destructive group, such as a drug syndicate, a group of bookies, or a subversive political party. There is usually a consensus of objectives and goals shared by the membership, and their behavior tends to be essentially organized group action.

The structure of a near-group is such that its functions not only vary greatly and shift considerably from time to time, but its primary function is unclear. The gang may on one occasion be organized to protect the neighborhood; on another occasion, to take over a particular territory; and on still another, it may be organized in response to or for the purpose of racial discrimination.

The function of near-groups, moreover, is not one which is clearly understood, known, and communicated among all of its members. There is no consensus in this near-group of goals, objectives, or functions of the collectivity—much near-group behavior is individualistic and flows from emotional disturbance.

A prime function of the gang is to provide a channel to act out hostility and aggression to satisfy the continuing and momentary emotional needs of its members. The gang is a convenient and malleable structure quickly adaptable to the needs of emotionally disturbed youths, who are unable to fulfill the responsibility and demands required for participation in constructive groups. He belongs to the gang because he lacks the social ability to relate to others and to assume responsibility for the relationship, not because the gang gives him a "feeling of belonging."

Because of the gang youth's limited "social ability," he constructs a social organization which enables him to relate and to function at his limited level of performance. In this structure norms are adjusted so that the gang youth can function and achieve despite his limited ability to relate to others.

An example of this is the function of violence in the near-group of the gang. Violence in the gang is highly valued as a means for the achievement of reputation or "rep." This inversion of societal norms is a means for quick upward social mobility in the gang. He can acquire and maintain a position in the gang through establishing a violent reputation. . . .

The near-group of the gang, with its diffuse and malleable structure, can function as a convenient vehicle for the acting out of varied individual needs and problems. For the gang leader it can be a super-powered organization through which (in his phantasy) he dominates and controls "divisions" of thousands of members. For gang members, unable to achieve in more demanding social organizations, swift and sudden violence is a means for quick upward social mobility and the achievement of a reputation. For less disturbed youths, the gang may function as a convenient temporary escape from the dull and rigid requirements of a difficult and demanding society. These are only some of the functions the near-group of the gang performs for its membership.

NEAR-GROUP THEORY AND SOCIAL PROBLEMS

The concept of the near-group may be of importance in the analysis of other collectivities which reflect and produce social problems. The analysis of other social structures may reveal similar distortions of their organization. To operate on an assumption that individuals in interaction with each other, around some function, with some shared mutual expectation, in a particular normative system as always being a group formation is to project a degree of distortion onto certain types of collectivities. Groups are social structures at one end of a continuum; mobs are social structures at another end; and at the center are near-groups which have some of the characteristics of both, and yet are characterized by factors not found fully in either.

In summary, these factors may include the following:
(1) Individualized role definition to fit momentary needs.
(2) Diffuse and differential definitions of membership.
(3) Emotion-motivated behavior.
(4) A decrease of cohesiveness as one moves from the center of the collectivity to the periphery.
(5) Limited responsibility and sociability required for membership and belonging.
(6) Self-appointed and disturbed leadership.
(7) A limited consensus among participants of the collectivities' functions or goals.
(8) A shifting and personalized stratification system.
(9) Shifting membership.
(10) The inclusion in size of phantasy membership.
(11) Limited consensus of normative expectations.
(12) Norms in conflict with the inclusive social system's prescriptions.

Although the gang was the primary type of near-group appraised in this analysis, there are perhaps other collectivities whose structure is distorted by autistic observers. Their organization might become clearer if subjected to this conceptual scheme. Specifically, in the area of criminal behavior, these might very well include adult gangs varyingly called the "Mafia," the "National Crime Syndicate," and so-called International Crime Cartels. There are indications that these social organizations are comparable in organization to the delinquent gang. They might fit the near-group category if closely analyzed in this context, rather than aggrandized and distorted by mass media and even Senate Committees.

Other more institutionalized collectivities might fit the near-group pattern. As a possible example, "the family in transition" may not be in transition at all. The family, as a social institution, may be suffering from near-groupism. Moreover, such standardized escape hatches of alcoholism, psychoses, and addictions may be too prosaic for the sophisticated intellectual to utilize in escape from himself. For him, the creation and perpetuation of near-groups requiring limited responsibility and personal commitment may be a more attractive contemporary form for expressing social and personal pathology. The measure of organization or disorganization of an inclusive social system may possibly be assessed by the prevalence of near-group collectivities in its midst. The delinquent gang may be only one type of near-group in American society.

FOOTNOTES

[1] Albert K. Cohen, *Delinquent Boys,* Glencoe: The Free Press, 1955.
[2] Herbert Block, and Arthur Nederhoffer, *The Gang,* New York: The Philosophical Library, 1958.
[3] New York Newspaper Headlines, June 11, 1955.
[4] Slyvan S. Furman, *Reaching the Unreached,* New York: Youth Board, 1952, p. 107.

5

LOWER CLASS CULTURE AS A GENERATING MILIEU OF GANG DELINQUENCY

Walter B. Miller

The etiology of delinquency has long been a controversial issue, and is particularly so at present. As new frames of reference for explaining human behavior have been added to traditional theories, some authors have adopted the practice of citing the major postulates of each school of thought as they pertain to delinquency, and going on to state that causality must be conceived in terms of the dynamic interaction of a complex combination of variables on many levels. The major sets of etiological factors currently adduced to explain delinquency are, in simplified terms, the physiological (delinquency results from organic pathology), the psychodynamic (delinquency is a "behavioral disorder" resulting primarily from emotional disturbance generated by a defective mother-child relationship), and the

Reprinted with permission of the author and publisher, from *Journal of Social Issues*, Volume 14, Number 3, pp. 5-19.

environmental (delinquency is the product of disruptive forces, "disorganization," in the actor's physical or social environment).

This paper selects one particular kind of "delinquency"[1] —law-violating acts committed by members of adolescent street corner groups in lower class communities—and attempts to show that the dominant component of motivation underlying these acts consists in a directed attempt by the actor to adhere to forms of behavior, and to achieve standards of value as they are defined within that community. It takes as a premise that the motivation of behavior in this situation can be approached most productively by attempting to understand the nature of cultural forces impinging on the acting individual as they are perceived *by the actor himself*—although by no means only that segment of these forces of which the actor is consciously aware—rather than as they are perceived and evaluated from the reference position of another cultural system. In the case of "gang" delinquency, the cultural system which exerts the most direct influence on behavior is that of the lower class community itself—a long-established, distinctively patterned tradition with an integrity of its own—rather than a so-called "delinquent subculture" which has arisen through conflict with middle class culture and is oriented to the deliberate violation of middle class norms.

The bulk of the substantive data on which the following material is based was collected in connection with a service-research project in the control of gang delinquency. During the service aspect of the project, which lasted for three years, seven trained social workers maintained contact with twenty-one corner group units in a "slum" district of a large eastern city for periods of time ranging from ten to thirty months. Groups were Negro and white, male and female, and in early, middle, and late adolescence. Over eight thousand pages of direct observational data on behavior patterns of group members and other community residents were collected; almost daily contact was maintained for a total time period of about thirteen worker years. Data include workers' contact reports, participant observation reports by the writer—a cultural anthropologist—and direct tape recordings of group activities and discussions.[2]

FOCAL CONCERNS OF LOWER CLASS CULTURE

There is a substantial segment of present-day American society whose way of life, values, and characteristic patterns of behavior are the product of a distinctive cultural system which may be termed "lower class." Evidence indicates that this cultural system is becoming increasingly distinctive, and that the size of the group which shares this tradition is increasing.[3] The lower class way of life, in common with that of all distinctive cultural groups, is characterized by a set of focal concerns—areas or issues which command widespread and persistent attention and a high degree of emotional involvement. The specific concerns cited here, while by no means confined to the American lower classes, constitute a distinctive *patterning* of concerns which differs significantly, both in rank order and weighting from that of American middle class culture. The following chart presents a highly schematic and simplified listing of six of the major concerns of lower class culture. Each is conceived as a "dimension" within which a fairly wide and varied range of alternative behavior patterns may be followed by different individuals under different situations. They are listed roughly in order of the degree of *explicit* attention accorded each, and, in this sense represent a weighted ranking of concerns. The "perceived alternatives" represent polar positions which define certain parameters within each dimension. As will be explained in more detail, it is necessary in relating the influence of these "concerns" to the motivation of delinquent behavior to specify *which* of its aspects is oriented to, whether orientation is *overt* or *covert, positive* (conforming to or seeking the aspect), or *negative* (rejecting or seeking to avoid the aspect).

The concept "focal concern" is used here in preference to the concept "value" for several interrelated reasons: (1) It is more readily derivable from direct field observation. (2) It is descriptively neutral—permitting independent consideration of positive and negative valences as varying under different conditions, whereas "value" carries a built-in positive valence. (3) It makes possible more refined analysis of subcultural differences, since it reflects actual behavior, whereas "value" tends to wash out intracultural differences since it is colored by notions of the "official" ideal. . . .

CHART 1
Focal Concerns of Lower Class Culture

Area	Perceived Alternatives (state, quality, condition)	
1. *Trouble:*	law-abiding behavior	law-violating behavior
2. *Toughness:*	physical prowess, skill; "masculinity"; fearlessness, bravery, daring	weakness, ineptitude; effeminacy; timidity, cowardice, caution
3. *Smartness:*	ability to outsmart, dupe, "con"; gaining money by "wits"; shrewdness, adroitness in repartee	gullibility, "con-ability"; gaining money by hard work; slowness, dull-wittedness, verbal maladroitness
4. *Excitement:*	thrill; risk, danger; change, activity	boredom; "deadness," safeness; sameness, passivity
5. *Fate:*	favored by fortune, being	ill-omened, being "unlucky"
6. *Autonomy:*	freedom from external constraint; freedom from superordinate authority; independence	presence of external constraint; presence of strong authority; dependency, being "cared for"

FOCAL CONCERNS OF THE LOWER CLASS ADOLESCENT STREET CORNER GROUP

The one-scx peer group is a highly prevalent and significant structural form in the lower class community. There is a strong probability that the prevalence and stability of this type of unit is directly related to the prevalence of a stabilized type of lower class child-rearing unit—the "female-based" household. This is a nuclear kin unit in which a male parent is either absent from the household, present only sporadically, or, when present, only minimally or inconsistently involved in the support and rearing of children. This unit usually consists of one or more females of child-bearing age and their offspring. The females are frequently related to one another by blood or marriage ties, and the unit often includes two or more generations of women, e.g., the mother and/or aunt or the principal child-bearing female.

The nature of social groupings in the lower class community may be clarified if we make the assumption that it is the *one-sex peer unit* rather than the two-parent family unit which represents the most significant relational unit for both sexes in lower class communities. Lower class society may be pictured as comprising a set of age-graded one-sex groups which constitute the major psychic focus and reference group for those over twelve or thirteen. Men and women of mating age leave these groups periodically to form temporary marital alliances, but these lack stability, and after varying periods of "trying out" the two-sex family arrangement, gravitate back to the more "comfortable" one-sex grouping, whose members exert strong pressure on the individual *not* to disrupt the group by adopting a two-sex household pattern of life.[4] Membership in a stable and solidary peer unit is vital to the lower class individual precisely to the extent to which a range of essential functions—psychological, educational, and others, are not provided by the "family" unit.

The adolescent street corner group represents the adolescent variant of this lower class structural form. What has been called the "delinquent gang" is one subtype of this form, defined on the basis of frequency of participation in law-violating activity; this subtype should not be considered a legitimate unit of study per se, but rather as one particular variant of the adolescent street corner group. The "hanging" peer group is a unit of particular importance for the adolescent male. In many cases it is the most stable and solidary primary group he has ever belonged to; for boys reared in female-based households the corner group provides the first real opportunity to learn essential aspects of the male role in the context of peers facing similar problems of sex-role identification.

The form and functions of the adolescent corner group operate as a selective mechanism in recruiting members. The activity patterns of the group require a high level of intra-group solidarity; individual members must possess a good capacity for subordinating individual desires to general group interests as well as the capacity for intimate and persisting interaction. Thus highly "disturbed" individuals, or those who cannot tolerate consistently imposed sanctions on "deviant" behavior cannot remain accepted members; the group itself will extrude those whose behavior exceeds limits defined as "normal." This selective process produces a type of group whose members possess to an unusually high degree both the *capacity* and *motivation* to conform to perceived cultural norms, so that the nature of the system of norms and values oriented to is a particularly influential component of motivation.

Focal concerns of the male adolescent corner group are those of the general cultural milieu in which it functions. As would be expected, the relative weighting and importance of these concerns pattern somewhat differently for adolescents than for adults. The nature of this patterning centers around two additional "concerns" of particular importance to this group—concern with "belonging," and with "status." These may be conceptualized as being on a higher level of abstraction than concerns previously cited, since "status" and "belonging" are achieved *via* cited concern areas of Toughness, etc. . . .

LOWER CLASS CULTURE AND THE
MOTIVATION OF DELINQUENT BEHAVIOR

The customary set of activities of the adolescent street corner group includes activities which are in violation of laws and ordinances of the legal code. Most of these center around assault and theft of various types (the gang fight; auto theft; assault on an individual; petty pilfering and shoplifting; "mugging"; pocketbook theft). Members of street corner gangs are well aware of the law-violating nature of these acts; they are not psychopaths, nor physically or mentally "defective"; in fact, since the corner group supports and enforces a rigorous set of standards which demand a high degree of fitness and personal competence, it tends to recruit from the most "able" members of the community.

Why, then, is the commission of crimes a customary feature of gang activity? The most general answer is that the commission of crimes by members of adolescent street corner groups is motivated primarily by the attempt to achieve ends, states, or conditions which are valued, and to avoid those that are disvalued within their most meaningful cultural milieu, through those culturally available avenues which appear as the most feasible means of attaining those ends.

The operation of these influences is well illustrated by the gang fight—a prevalent and characteristic type of corner group delinquency. This type of activity comprises a highly stylized and culturally patterned set of sequences. Although details vary under different circumstances, the following events are generally included. A member or several members of group A "trespass" on the claimed territory of group B. While there they commit an act or acts which group B defines as a violation of its rightful privileges, an affront to their honor, or a challenge to their "rep." Frequently this act involves advances to a girl associated with group B; it may occur at a dance or party; sometimes the mere act of "trespass" is seen as deliberate provocation. Members of group B then assault members of group A, if they are caught while still in B's territory. Assaulted members of group A return to their "home" territory and recount to members of their group details of the incident, stressing the insufficient nature of the provocation ("I just *looked* at her! Hardly even said anything!"), and the unfair circumstances of the assault ("About *twenty* guys jumped just the *two* of us!"). The highly colored account is acutely inflammatory; group A, perceiving its honor violated and its "rep" threatened, feels obligated to retaliate in force. Sessions of detailed planning now occur; allies are recruited if the size of group A and its potential allies appears to necessitate larger numbers; strategy is plotted, and messengers dispatched. Since the prospect of a gang fight is frightening to even the "toughest" group members, a constant rehearsal of the provocative incident or incidents and the essentially evil nature of the opponents accompanies the planning process to bolster possibly weakening motivation to fight. The excursion into "enemy" territory sometimes results in a full scale fight; more often group B cannot be found, or the police appear and stop the fight, "tipped off" by an anonymous informant. When this occurs, group members express disgust and disappointment; secretly there is much relief; their honor has been avenged without incurring injury; often the anonymous tipster is a member of one of the involved groups.

The basic elements of this type of delinquency are sufficiently stabilized and recurrent as to constitute an essentially ritualized pattern, resembling both in structure and expressed motives for action classic forms such as the European "duel," the American Indian tribal war, and the Celtic clan feud. Although the arousing and "acting out" of individual aggressive emotions are inevitably involved in the gang fight, neither its form nor motivational dynamics can be adequately handled within a predominantly personality-focused frame of reference.

It would be possible to develop in considerable detail the processes by which the commission of a range of illegal acts is either explicitly supported by, implicitly demanded by, or not materially inhibited by factors relating to the focal concerns of lower class culture. In place of such a development, the following three statements condense in general terms the operation of these processes:

1. *Following cultural practices which comprise essential elements of the total life pattern of lower class culture automatically violates certain legal norms.*
2. *In instances where alternate avenues to similar objectives are available, the non-law-abiding avenue frequently provides a relatively greater and more immediate return for a relatively smaller investment of energy.*
3. *The "demanded" response to certain situations recurrently engendered within lower class culture involves the commission of illegal acts.*

The primary thesis of this paper is that the dominant component of the motivation of "delinquent" behavior engaged in by members of lower class corner groups involves a positive effort to achieve states, conditions, or qualities valued within the actor's most significant cultural milieu. If "conformity to immediate reference group values" is the major component of motivation of "delinquent" behavior by gang members, why is such behavior frequently referred to as negativistic, malicious, or rebellious? Albert Cohen, for example, in *Delinquent Boys* (Glencoe: Free Press, 1955) describes behavior which violates school rules as comprising elements of "active spite and malice, contempt and ridicule, challenge and defiance." He ascribes to the gang "keen delight in terrorizing 'good' children, and in general making themselves obnoxious to the virtuous." A recent national conference on social work with "hard-to-reach" groups characterized lower class corner groups as "youth groups in conflict with the culture of their (*sic*) communities." Such characterizations are obviously the result of taking the middle class community and its institutions as an implicit point of reference.

A large body of systematically interrelated attitudes, practices, behaviors, and values characteristic of lower class culture are designed to support and maintain the basic features of the lower class way of life. In areas where these differ from features of middle class culture, action oriented to the achievement and maintenance of the lower class system may violate norms of middle class culture and be perceived as deliberately non-conforming or malicious by an observer strongly cathected to middle class norms. This does not mean, however, that violation of the middle class norm is the dominant component of motivation; it is a by-product of action primarily oriented to the lower class system. The standards of lower class culture cannot be seen merely as a reverse function of middle class culture—as middle class standards "turned upside down"; lower class culture is a distinctive tradition many centuries old with an integrity of its own.

From the viewpoint of the acting individual, functioning within a field of well-structured cultural forces, the relative impact of "conforming" and "rejective" elements in the motivation of gang delinquency is weighted preponderantly on the conforming side. Rejective or rebellious elements are inevitably involved, but their influence during the actual commission of delinquent acts is relatively small compared to the influence of pressures to achieve what is valued by the actor's most immediate reference groups. Expressed awareness by the actor of the element of rebellion often represents only that aspect of motivation of which he is explicitly conscious; the deepest and most compelling components of motivation—adherence to highly meaningful group standards of Toughness, Smartness, Excitement, etc.—are often unconsciously patterned. No cultural pattern as well-established as the practice of illegal acts by members of lower class corner groups could persist if buttressed primarily by negative, hostile, or rejective motives; its principal motivational support, as in the case of any persisting cultural tradition, derives from a positive effort to achieve what is valued within that tradition, and to conform to its explicit and implicit norms.

FOOTNOTES

[1]The complex issues involved in deriving a definition of "delinquency" cannot be discussed here. The term "delinquent" is used in this paper to characterize behavior or acts committed by individuals within specified age limits which if known to official authorities could result in legal action. The concept of a "delinquent" individual has little or no utility in the approach used here; rather, specified types of *acts* which may be committed rarely or frequently by few or many individuals are characterized as "delinquent."

[2]A three year research project is being financed under National Institutes of Health Grant M–1414, and administered through the Boston University School of Social Work. . . .

[3]Between 40 and 60 per cent of all Americans are directly influenced by lower class culture, with about 15 per cent, or twenty-five million, comprising the "hard core" lower class group–defined primarily by its use of the "female-based" household as the basic form of child-rearing unit and of the "serial monogamy" mating pattern as the primary form of marriage. The term "lower class culture" as used here refers most specifically to the way of life of the "hard core" group; systematic research in this area would probably reveal at least four to six major subtypes of lower class culture, for some of which the "concerns" presented here would be differently weighted, especially for those subtypes in which "law-abiding" behavior has a high overt valuation. It is impossible within the compass of this short paper to make the finer intra-cultural distinctions which a more accurate presentation would require.

[4]Further data on the female-based household unit (estimated as comprising about 15 per cent of all American "families") and the role of one-sex groupings in lower class culture are contained in Walter B. Miller, "Implications of Urban Lower Class Culture for Social Work," *Social Service Review* (1959), No. 3.

6

THIEVES, CONVICTS AND
THE INMATE CULTURE

John Irwin and Donald R. Cressey

In the rapidly-growing literature on the social organization of correctional institutions, it has become common to discuss "prison culture" and "inmate culture" in terms suggesting that the behavior systems of various types of inmates stem from the conditions of imprisonment themselves. Use of a form of structural-functional analysis in research and observation of institutions has led to emphasis of the notion that internal conditions stimulate inmate behavior of various kinds, and there has been a glossing over of the older notion that inmates may bring a culture with them into the prison. Our aim is to suggest that much of the inmate behavior classified as part of the prison culture is not peculiar to the prison at all. On the contrary, it is the fine distinction between "prison

Reprinted with permission of the authors and The Society for the Study of Social Problems, from *Social Problems*, Volume 10, Fall 1962, pp. 142-155.

culture" and "criminal subculture" which seems to make understandable the fine distinction between behavior patterns of various categories of inmates.

A number of recent publications have defended the notion that behavior patterns among inmates develop with a minimum of influence from the outside world. . . .

It is our contention that the "functional" or "indigenous origin" notion has been overemphasized and that observers have overlooked the dramatic effect that external behavior patterns have on the conduct of inmates in any given prison. Moreover, the contradictory statements made in this connection by some authors, including Cressey,[1] seem to stem from acknowledging but then ignoring the deviant subcultures which exist outside any given prison and outside prisons generally. More specifically, it seems rather obvious that the "prison code"—don't inform on or exploit another inmate, don't lose your head, be weak, or be a sucker, etc.—is also part of a *criminal* code, existing outside prisons. Further, many inmates come to any given prison with a record of many terms in correctional institutions. These men, some of whom have institutional records dating back to early childhood, bring with them a ready-made set of patterns which they apply to the new situation, just as is the case with participants in the criminal subculture. In view of these variations, a clear understanding of inmate conduct cannot be obtained simply by viewing "prison culture" or "inmate culture" as an isolated system springing solely from the conditions of imprisonment. Becker and Geer have made our point in more general terms: "The members of a group may derive their understandings from cultures other than that of the group they are at the moment participating in. To the degree that group participants share latent social identities (related to their membership in the same 'outside' social groups) they will share these understandings, so that there will be a culture which can be called *latent*, i.e., the culture has its origin and social support in a group other than the one in which the members are now participating."[2]

We have no doubt that the total set of relationships called "inmate society" is a response to problems of imprisonment. What we question is the emphasis given to the notion that solutions to these problems are found within the prison, and the lack of emphasis on "latent culture"—on external experiences as determinants of the solutions. We have found it both necessary and helpful to divide inmates into three rough categories: those oriented to a criminal subculture, those oriented to a prison subculture, and those oriented to "conventional" or "legitimate" subcultures.

THE TWO DEVIANT SUBCULTURES

When we speak of a criminal subculture we do not mean to imply that there is some national or international organization with its own judges, enforcement agencies, etc. Neither do we imply that every person convicted of a crime is a member of the subculture. Nevertheless, descriptions of the values of professional thieves, "career criminals," "sophisticated criminals," and other good crooks indicate that there is a set of values which extends to criminals across the nation with a good deal of consistency.[3] To avoid possible confusion arising from the fact that not all criminals share these values, we have arbitrarily named the system a "thief" subculture. The core values of this subculture correspond closely to the values which prison observers have ascribed to the "right guy" role. These include the important notion that criminals should not betray each other to the police, should be reliable, wily but trustworthy, cool headed, etc. High status in this subculture is awarded to men who appear to follow these prescriptions without variance. In the thief subculture a man who is known as "right" or "solid" is one who can be trusted and relied upon. High status is also awarded to those who possess skill as thieves, but to be just a successful thief is not enough; there must be solidness as well. A solid guy is respected even if he is unskilled, and no matter how skilled in crime a stool pigeon may be, his status is low.

Despite the fact that adherence to the norms of the thief subculture is an ideal, and the fact that the behavior of the great majority of men arrested or convicted varies sharply from any "criminal code" which might be identified, a proportion of the persons arrested for "real crime" such as burglary, robbery, and larceny have been in close contact with the values of the subculture.

Many criminals, while not following the precepts of the subculture religiously, give lip service to its values and evaluate their own behavior and the behavior of their associates in terms relating to adherence to "rightness" and being "solid." It is probable, further, that use of this kind of values is not even peculiarly "criminal," for policemen, prison guards, college professors, students, and almost any other category of persons evaluate behavior in terms of in-group loyalties. Whyte noted the mutual obligations binding corner boys together and concluded that status depends upon the extent to which a boy lives up to his obligations, a form of "solidness."[4] More recently, Miller identified "toughness," "smartness," and "autonomy" among the "focal concerns" of lower class adolescent delinquent boys; these also characterize prisoners who are oriented to the thief subculture.[5] Wheeler found that half of the custody staff and sixty per cent of the treatment staff in one prison approved the conduct of a hypothetical inmate who refused to name an inmate with whom he had been engaged in a knife fight.[6] A recent book has given the name "moral courage" to the behavior of persons who, like thieves, have shown extreme loyalty to their in-groups in the face of real or threatened adversity, including imprisonment.[7]

Imprisonment is one of the recurring problems with which thieves must cope. It is almost certain that a thief will be arrested from time to time, and the subculture provides members with patterns to be used in order to help solve this problem. Norms which apply to the prison situation, and information on how to undergo the prison experience—how to do time "standing on your head"—with the least suffering and in a minimum amount of time are provided. Of course, the subculture itself is both nurtured and diffused in the different jails and prisons of the country.

There also exists in prisons a subculture which is by definition a set of patterns that flourishes in the environment of incarceration. It can be found wherever men are confined, whether it be in city jails, state and federal prisons, army stockades, prisoner of war camps, concentration camps, or even mental hospitals. Such organizations are characterized by deprivations and limitations on freedom, and in them available wealth must be competed for by men supposedly on an equal footing. It is in connection with the *maintenance* (but not necessarily with the *origin*) of this subculture that it is appropriate to stress the notion that a minimum of outside status criteria are carried into the situation. Ideally, all status is to be achieved by the means made available in the prison, through the displayed ability to manipulate the environment, win special privileges in a certain manner, and assert influence over others. To avoid confusion with writings on "prison culture" and "inmate culture," we have arbitrarily named this system of values and behavior patterns a "convict subculture." The central value of the subculture is utilitarianism, and the most manipulative and most utilitarian individuals win the available wealth and such positions of influence as might exist.

It is not correct to conclude, however, that even these behavior patterns are a consequence of the environment of any particular prison. In the first place, such utilitarian and manipulative behavior probably is characteristic of the "hard core" lower class in the United States, and most prisoners come from this class. After discussing the importance of toughness, smartness, excitement and fate in this group, Miller makes the following significant observation:

> *In lower class culture a close conceptual connection is made between "authority" and "nurturance." To be restrictively or firmly controlled is to be cared for. Thus the overtly negative evaluation of superordinate authority frequently extends as well to nurturance, care, or protection. The desire for personal independence is often expressed in terms such as "I don't need nobody to take care of me. I can take care of myself!" Actual patterns of behavior, however, reveal a marked discrepancy between expressed sentiments and what is covertly valued. Many lower class people appear to seek out highly restrictive social environments wherein stringent external controls are maintained over their behavior. Such institutions as the armed forces, the mental hospital, the disciplinary school, the prison or correctional institution, provide environments which incorporate a strict and detailed set of rules defining and limiting behavior, and enforced by an authority system which controls and applies coercive sanctions for deviance from these rules. While under the jurisdiction of such systems, the lower*

class person generally expresses to his peers continual resent-ment of the coercive, unjust, and arbitrary exercise of author-ity. Having been released, or having escaped from these milieux, however, he will often act in such a way as to insure recommitment, or choose recommitment voluntarily after a temporary period of "freedom."[8]

In the second place, the "hard core" members of this subculture as it exists in American prisons for adults are likely to be inmates who have a long record of confinement in institutions for juveniles. McCleery observed that, in a period of transition, reform-school graduates all but took over inmate society in one prison. These boys called themselves a "syndicate" and engaged in a concentrated campaign of argument and intimidation directed toward capturing the inmate council and the inmate craft shop which had been placed under council management. "The move of the syndicate to take over the craft shop involved elements of simple exploitation, the grasp for a status symbol, and an aspect of economic reform."[9] Persons with long histories of institutionalization, it is important to note, might have had little contact with the thief subculture. The thief subculture does not flourish in institutions for juveniles, and graduates of such institutions have not necessarily had extensive criminal experience on the outside. However, some form of the convict subculture *does* exist in institutions for juveniles, though not to the extent characterizing prisons for felons. Some of the newcomers to a prison for adults are, in short, persons who have been oriented to the convict subculture, who have found the utilitarian nature of this subculture acceptable, and who have had little contact with the thief subculture. This makes a difference in their behavior.

The category of inmates we have characterized as oriented to "legitimate" subcultures includes men who are not members of the thief subculture upon entering prison and who reject both the thief subculture and the convict subculture while in prison. These men present few problems to prison administrators. They make up a large percentage of the population of any prison, but they isolate them-selves—or are isolated—from the thief and convict subcultures. Clemmer found that forty per cent of a sample of the men in his prison did not consider themselves a part of any group, and another forty per cent could be considered a member of a "semi-primary group" only.[10] He referred to these men as "ungrouped," and his statistics have often been interpreted as meaning that the prison contains many men not oriented to "inmate culture" or "prison culture"—in our terms, not oriented to either the thief subculture or the convict subculture. This is not necessarily the case. There may be sociometric isolates among the thief-oriented prisoners, the convict-oriented prisoners, and the legitimately oriented prisoners. Consequently, we have used the "legitimate subcultures" terminology rather than Clemmer's term "ungrouped." Whether or not men in this category participate in cliques, athletic teams, or religious study and hobby groups, they are oriented to the problem of achieving goals through means which are legitimate outside prisons.

BEHAVIOR PATTERNS IN PRISON

On an ideal-type level, there are great differences in the prison behavior of men oriented to one or the other of the three types of subculture. The hard core member of the convict subculture finds his reference groups inside the institutions and, as indicated, he seeks status through means available in the prison environment. But it is important for the understanding of inmate conduct to note that the hard core member of the thief subculture seeks status in the broader criminal world of which prison is only a part. His reference groups include people both inside and outside prison, but he is committed to criminal life, not prison life. From his point of view, it is adherence to a widespread criminal code that wins him high status, not adherence to a narrower convict code. Convicts might assign him high status because they admire him as a thief, or because a good thief makes a good convict, but the thief does not play the convicts' game. Similarly, a man oriented to a legitimate subculture is by definition committed to the values of neither thieves nor convicts.

On the other hand, within any given prison, the men oriented to the convict subculture are the inmates that seek positions of power, influence, and sources of information, whether these men are called "shots," "politicians," "merchants," "hoods," "toughs," "gorillas," or something else. A job as secretary to the Captain or Warden, for example, gives an aspiring prisoner information and consequent power, and enables him to influence the assignment or regulation of other inmates. In the same way, a job which allows the incumbent to participate in a racket, such as clerk in the kitchen storeroom where he can steal and sell food, is highly desirable to a man oriented to the convict subculture. With a steady income of cigarettes, ordinarily the prisoners' medium of exchange, he may assert a great deal of influence and purchase those things which are symbols of status among persons oriented to the convict subculture. Even if there is no well-developed medium of exchange, he can barter goods acquired in his position for equally-desirable goods possessed by other convicts. These include information and such things as specially-starched, pressed, and tailored prison clothing, fancy belts, belt buckles or billfolds, special shoes, or any other type of dress which will set him apart and will indicate that he has both the influence to get the goods and the influence necessary to keeping and displaying them despite prison rules which outlaw doing so. In California, special items of clothing, and clothing that is neatly laundered, are called "bonaroos" (a corruption of *bonnet rouge,* by means of which French prison trustics were once distinguished from the common run of prisoners), and to a lesser degree even the persons who wear such clothing are called "bonaroos."

Two inmates we observed in one prison are somewhat representative of high status members of the convict subculture. One was the prison's top gambler, who bet the fights, baseball games, football games, ran pools, etc. His cell was always full of cigarettes, although he did not smoke. He had a job in the cell block taking care of the laundry room, and this job gave him time to conduct his gambling activities. It also allowed him to get commissions for handling the clothing of inmates who paid to have them "bonarooed," or who had friends in the laundry who did this for them free of charge, in return for some service. The "commissions" the inmate received for doing this service were not always direct; the "favors" he did gave him influence with many of the inmates in key jobs, and he reputedly could easily arrange cell changes and job changes. Shortly after he was paroled he was arrested and returned to prison for robbing a liquor store. The other inmate was the prison's most notorious "fag" or "queen." He was feminine in appearance and gestures, and wax had been injected under the skin on his chest to give the appearance of breasts. At first he was kept in a cell block isolated from the rest of the prisoners, but later he was released out into the main population. He soon went to work in a captain's office, and became a key figure in the convict subculture. He was considered a stool pigeon by the thieves, but he held high status among participants in the convict subculture. In the first place, he was the most desired fag in the prison. In the second place, he was presumed to have considerable influence with the officers who frequented the captain's office. He "married" another prisoner, who also was oriented to the convict subculture.

Since prisoners oriented either to a legitimate subculture or to a thief subculture are not seeking high status within any given prison, they do not look for the kinds of positions considered so desirable by the members of the convict subculture. Those oriented to legitimate subcultures take prison as it comes and seek status through channels provided for that purpose by prison administrators—running for election to the inmate council, to the editorship of the institutional newspaper, etc.—and by, generally, conforming to what they think administrators expect of "good prisoners." Long before the thief has come to prison, his subculture has defined proper prison conduct as behavior rationally calculated to "do time" in the easiest possible way. This means that he wants a prison life containing the best possible combination of a maximum amount of leisure time and a maximum number of privileges. Accordingly, the privileges sought by the thief are different from the privileges sought by the man oriented to prison itself. The thief wants things that will make prison life a little easier—extra food, a maximum amount of recreation time, a good radio, a little peace. One thief serving his third sentence for armed robbery was a dish washer in the officers' dining room. He liked the eating privileges, but he never sold food. Despite his "low status" job, he was highly respected by other thieves, who described him as "right," and "solid." Members of the convict subculture, like the thieves, seek privileges. There is a difference, however, for the convict seeks privileges which he believes will enhance his position in the inmate hierarchy. He also wants to do easy time but, as compared with the thief, desirable privileges are more likely to involve freedom to amplify one's store, such as stealing rights in the kitchen, and freedom of movement around the prison. Obtaining an easy job is managed because it is easy and therefore desirable, but it also is managed for the purpose of displaying the fact that it can be obtained.

In one prison, a man serving his second sentence for selling narcotics (he was not an addict) worked in the bakery during the entire term of his sentence. To him, a thief, this was a "good job," for the hours were short and the bakers ate very well. There were some rackets conducted from the bakery, such as selling cocoa, but the man never participated in these activities. He was concerned a little with learning a trade, but not very seriously. Most of all, he wanted the eating privileges which the bakery offered. A great deal of his time was spent reading psychology, philosophy, and mysticism. Before his arrest he had been a reader of tea leaves and he now was working up some plans for an illegal business involving mysticism. Other than this, his main activity was sitting with other inmates and debating.

Just as both thieves and convicts seek privileges, both seek the many kinds of contraband in a prison. But again the things the thief seeks are those that contribute to an easier life, such as mechanical gadgets for heating water for coffee and cocoa, phonographs and radios if they are contraband or not, contraband books, food, writing materials, socks, etc. He may "score" for food occasionally (unplanned theft in which advantage is taken of a momentary opportunity), but he does not have a "route" (highly organized theft of food). One who "scores" for food eats it, shares it with his friends, sometimes in return for a past or expected favors, but he does not sell it. One who has a "route" is in the illicit food selling business.[11] The inmate oriented to the convict subculture, with its emphasis on displaying ability to manipulate the environment, rather than on pleasure, is the inmate with the "route." The difference is observable in the case of an inmate assigned to the job of clerk in the dental office of one prison. This man was known to both inmates and staff long before he arrived at the institution, for his crime and arrest were highly publicized in the newspapers. It also became known that he had done time in another penitentiary for "real crime," and that his criminal exploits had frequently taken him from one side of the United States to the other. His assignment to the dental office occurred soon after he entered the prison, and some of the inmates believed that such a highly-desirable job could not be achieved without "influence" and "rep." It was an ideal spot for conducting a profitable business, and a profitable business was in fact being conducted there. In order to get on the list to see the dentist, an inmate had to pay a price in cigarettes to two members of the convict subculture who were running the dental office. This practice soon changed, at least in reference to inmates who could show some contact with our man's criminal friends, in or out of prison. If a friend vouched for a man by saying he was "right" or "solid" the man would be sitting in the dental chair the next day, free of charge.

Generally speaking, an inmate oriented to the thief subculture simply is not interested in gaining high status in the prison. He wants to get out. Moreover, he is likely to be quietly amused by the concern some prisoners have for symbols of status, but he publicly exhibits neither disdain nor enthusiasm for this concern. One exception to this occurred in an institution where a thief had become a fairly close friend of an inmate oriented to the prison. One day the latter showed up in a fresh set of bonaroos, and he made some remark that called attention to them. The thief looked at him, laughed, and said, "For Christ's sake, Bill, they're *Levi's* (standard prison blue denims) and they are always going to be Levi's." The thief may be accorded high status in the prison, because "rightness" is revered there as well as on the outside, but to him this is incidental to his being a "man," not to his being a prisoner.

Members of both subcultures are conservative—they want to maintain the status quo. Motivation is quite different, however. The man oriented to the convict subculture is conservative because he has great stock in the existing order of things, while the man who is thief oriented leans toward conservatism because he knows how to do time and likes things to run along smoothly with a minimum of friction. It is because of this conservatism that so many inmates are directly or indirectly in accommodation with prison officials who, generally speaking, also wish to maintain the status quo. A half dozen prison observers have recently pointed out that some prison leaders—those oriented to what we call the convict subculture—assist the officials by applying pressures that keep other inmates from causing trouble, while other prison leaders—those oriented to what we call the thief subculture—indirectly keep order by propagating the *criminal* code, including admonitions to "do your own time," "don't interfere with others' activities," "don't 'rank' another criminal." The issue is not whether the thief subculture and convict subculture are useful to, and used by, administrators; it is whether the observed behavior patterns originate in prison as a response to official administrative practices.

There are other similarities, noted by many observers of "prison culture" or "inmate culture." In the appropriate circumstances, members of both subcultures will participate in fomenting and carrying out riots. The man oriented to the convict subculture does this when a change has closed some of the paths for achieving positions of influence, but the thief does it when privileges of the kind that make life easier are taken away from him. Thus, when a "prison reform" group takes over an institution, it may inadvertently make changes which lead to alliances between the members of two subcultures who ordinarily are quite indifferent to each other. In more routine circumstances, the thief adheres to a tight system of mutual aid for other thieves—persons who are "right" and "solid"—a direct application in prison of the norms which ask that a thief prove himself reliable and trustworthy to other thieves. If a man is "right," then even if he is a stranger one must help him if there is no risk to himself. If he is a friend, then one must, in addition, be willing to take *some* risk in order to help him. But in the convict subculture, "help" has a price; one helps in order to gain, whether the gain be "pay" in the form of cigarettes, or a guarantee of a return favor which will enlarge one's area of power.

RELATIONSHIPS BETWEEN THE TWO SUBCULTURES

In the routine prison setting, the two deviant subcultures exist in a balanced relationship. It is this total setting which has been observed as "inmate culture." There is some conflict because of the great disparity in some of the values of thieves and convicts, but the two subcultures share other values. The thief is committed to keeping his hands off other people's activities, and the convict, being utilitarian, is likely to know that it is better in the long run to avoid conflict with thieves and confine one's exploitations to the "do rights" and to the members of his own subculture. Of course, the thief must deal with the convict from time to time, and when he does so he adjusts to the reality of the fact that he is imprisoned. Choosing to follow prison definitions usually means paying for some service in cigarettes or in a returned service; this is the cost of doing easy time. Some thieves adapt in a more general way to the ways of convicts and assimilate the prisonized person's concern for making out in the institution. On an ideal-type level, however, thieves do not sanction exploitation of other inmates, and they simply ignore the "do rights," who are oriented to legitimate subcultures. Nevertheless, their subculture as it operates in prison has exploitative effects.[12]

Numerous persons have documented the fact that "right guys," many of whom can be identified as leaders of the thieves, not of the convicts, exercise the greatest influence over the total prison population. The influence is the long run kind stemming from the ability to influence notions of what is right and proper, what McCleery calls the formulation and communication of definitions.[13] The thief, after all, has the respect of many inmates who are not themselves thieves. The right guy carries a set of attitudes, values and norms that have a great deal of consistency and clarity. He acts, forms opinions, and evaluates events in the prison according to them, and over a long period of time he in this way determines basic behavior patterns in the institution. In what the thief thinks of as "small matters," however—getting job transfers, enforcing payment of gambling debts, making cell assignments—members of the convict subculture run things.

It is difficult to assess the direct lines of influence the two deviant subcultures have over those inmates who are not members of either subculture when they enter a prison. It is true that if a new inmate does not have definitions to apply to the new prison situation, one or the other of the deviant subcultures is likely to supply them. On the one hand, the convict subculture is much more apparent than the thief subculture; its roles are readily visible to any new arrival, and its definitions are readily available to one who wants to "get along" and "make it" in a prison. Moreover, the inmate leaders oriented to the convict subculture are anxious to get new followers who will recognize the existing status hierarchy in the prison. Thieves, on the other hand, tend to be snobs. Their status in prison is determined in part by outside criteria, as well as by prison conduct, and it is therefore difficult for a prisoner, acting as a prisoner, to achieve these criteria. At a minimum, the newcomer can fall under the influence of the thief subculture only if he has intimate association over a period of time with some of its members who are able and willing to impart some of its subtle behavior patterns to him.

Our classification of some inmates as oriented to legitimate subcultures implies that many inmates entering a prison do not find either set of definitions acceptable to them. Like thieves, these men are not necessarily "stripped" of outside statuses, and they do not play the prison game. They bring a set of values with them when they come to prison, and they do not leave these values at the gate. They are people such as a man who, on a drunken Saturday night, ran over a pedestrian and was sent to the prison for manslaughter, a middle class clerk who was caught embezzling his firm's money, and a young soldier who stole a car in order to get back from a leave. Unlike thieves, these inmates bring to the prison both anti-criminal and anti-prisoner attitudes. Although it is known that most of them participate at a minimum in primary group relations with either thieves or convicts, their relationships with each other have not been studied. Further, criminologists have ignored the possible effects the "do rights" have on the total system of "inmate culture." It seems a worthy hypothesis that thieves, convicts and do rights all bring certain values and behavior patterns to prison with them, and that total "inmate culture" represents an adjustment or accommodation of these three systems within the official administrative system of deprivation and control.[14] It is significant in this connection that Wheeler has not found in Norwegian prisons the normative order and cohesive bonds among inmates that characterize many American prisons. He observes that his data suggest "that the current functional interpretations of the inmate system in American institutions are not adequate," and that "general features of Norwegian society are imported into the prison and operate largely to offset any tendencies toward the formation of a solidary inmate group. . . ."[15]

BEHAVIOR AFTER RELEASE

If our crude typology is valid, it should be of some use for predicting the behavior of prisoners when they are released. However, it is important to note that in any given prison the two deviant subcultures are not necessarily as sharply separated as our previous discussion has implied. Most inmates are under the influence of *both* subcultures. Without realizing it, inmates who have served long prison terms are likely to move toward the middle, toward a compromise or balance between the directives coming from the two sources. A member of the convict subculture may come to see that thieves are the real men with the prestige; a member of the thief subculture or even a do right may lose his ability to sustain his status needs by outside criteria. Criminologists seem to have had difficulty in keeping the two kinds of influence separate, and we cannot expect all inmates to be more astute than the criminologists. The fact that time has a blending effect on the participants in the two deviant subcultures suggests that the subcultures themselves tend to blend together in some prisons. We have already noted that the thief subculture scarcely exists in some institutions for juveniles. It is probable also that in army stockades and in concentration camps this subculture is almost nonexistent. In places of short-term confinement, such as city and county jails, the convict subculture is dominant, for the thief subculture involves status distinctions that are not readily observable in a short period of confinement. At the other extreme, in prisons where only prisoners with long sentences are confined, the distinctions between the two subcultures are likely to be blurred. Probably the two subcultures exist in their purest forms in institutions holding inmates in their twenties, with varying sentences for a variety of criminal offenses. Such institutions, of course, are the "typical" prisons of the United States.

Despite these differences, in any prison the men oriented to legitimate subcultures should have a low recidivism rate, while the highest recidivism rate should be found among participants in the convict subculture. The hard core members of this subculture are being trained in manipulation, duplicity and exploitation, they are not sure they can make it on the outside, and even when they are on the outside they continue to use convicts as a reference group. This sometimes means that there will be a wild spree of crime and dissipation which takes the members of the convict subculture directly back to the prison. Members of the thief subculture, to whom prison life represented a pitfall in outside life, also should have a high recidivism rate. However, the thief sometimes "reforms" and tries to succeed in some life within the law. Such behavior, contrary to popular notions, is quite acceptable to other members of the thief subculture, so long as the new job and position are not "anti-criminal" and do not involve regular, routine, "slave labor." Suckers work, but a man who, like a thief, "skims it off the top" is not a sucker. At any rate, the fact that convicts, to a greater extent than thieves, tend to evaluate things from the perspective of the prison and to look upon discharge as a short vacation from prison life suggests that their recidivism rate should be higher than that of thieves. . . .

FOOTNOTES

[1]Edwin H. Sutherland and Donald R. Cressey, *Principles of Criminology,* Sixth edition, New York: Lippincott, 1960, 504–505.

[2]Howard S. Becker and Blanche Geer, "Latent Culture: A Note on the Theory of Latent Social Roles," *Administrative Science Quarterly* (September, 1960), 305–306. See also Alvin W. Gouldner, "Cosmopolitans and Locals: Toward an Analysis of Latent Social Roles," *Administrative Science Quarterly* (1957), 281–306 and (1958), 444–480.

[3]Walter C. Reckless, *The Crime Problem,* Second Edition, New York: Appleton-Century-Crofts, 1945, 144–145; 148–150; Edwin H. Sutherland, *The Professional Thief,* Chicago: University of Chicago Press, 1937.

[4]William Foote Whyte, "Corner Boys: A Study of Clique Behavior," *American Journal of Sociology* (March, 1941), 647–663.

[5]Walter B. Miller, "Lower Class Culture as a Generating Milieu of Gang Delinquency," *Journal of Social Issues* (1958), 5–19.

[6]Stanton Wheeler, "Role Conflict in Correctional Communities," Chapter 6 in Donald R. Cressey, ed., *The Prison: Studies in Institutional Organization and Change,* New York: Holt, Rinehart and Winston, 1961, 235.

[7]Compton Mackenzie, *Moral Courage,* London: Collins, 1962.

[8]*Op. cit.,* 12–13.

[9]Richard H. McCleery, "The Governmental Process and Informal Social Control," Chapter 4 in Cressey, *op. cit.,* 179.

[10]*Op. cit.,* 116–133.

[11]See Schrag, "Some Foundations for a Theory of Correction," Chapter 8 in Cressey, *op. cit.,* 343.

[12]See Donald R. Cressey, "Foreword," to Clemmer, *op. cit.,* vii–x.

[13]"The Governmental Process and Informal Social Control," *op. cit.,* 154.

[14]"But if latent culture can restrict the possibilities for the proliferation of the manifest culture, the opposite is also true. Manifest culture can restrict the operation of latent culture. The problems facing group members may be so pressing that, given the social context in which the group operates, the range of solutions that will be effective may be so limited as not to allow for influence of variations resulting from cultures associated with other identities." Becker and Geer, *op. cit.,* 308–309.

[15]Stanton Wheeler, "Inmate Culture in Prisons," Mimeographed report of the Laboratory of Social Relations, Harvard University, 1962, 18, 20, 21.

7

SUBCULTURE MARGINALITY

An implicit argument of this entire book is that the notion of subculture requires a central place in the conceptual framework of sociology. The argument of this chapter is that using the notion *by itself* would distort our analysis of social reality. To develop this argument it is first necessary to consider the relationship between diverse subcultures in a society. After this, I shall consider the relationship between subcultures and their members, and from this develop the concept of subculture marginality to supplement the basic concept of subculture.

I.

Most studies of subcultures have, understandably, dealt with just

Prepared for this volume.

one subculture at a time. An unfortunate consequence of this is that our notions of subcultures fail to take into account crucial aspects of subcultures that result from the innumerable social overlappings that make up the social world.

To correct this, let us take a look at the form which the world of subcultures takes. Are subcultures discrete or over-lapping? Are their boundaries clear or fuzzy? Do individuals belong to just one? Or many? Or can someone not belong to any at all? What is the relationship between subcultures and the "great culture"? To complete our frame of reference we need some picture of the articulation of subcultures that provides at least a working answer to these questions.

Maurer has described a model which presents one possible answer. He suggests:

> It is helpful if we visualize the dominant culture as bounded by a large circle, with these subcultures, projected as very small circles, clustering about the rim of the large one. Thus some of these circles will be largely within the dominant culture, some encysted wholly within it, some only slightly within it, and others barely touching the periphery so that for all practical purposes they are outside it.[1]

This type of model is prevalent among sociologists using the subculture concept to deal only with deviant subcultures, since it is easy to locate a dimension which separates the (deviant) subcultures from the (conventional) total culture. Maurer suggests, for example, that all subcultures are differentiated from the dominant culture by being parasitic.[2]

But this model has the fault of turning a convenient abstraction into a supposed picture of reality, of taking vague boundary lines and going over them with a heavy crayon. It is a natural outgrowth of the combination of a substantive focus on deviance with the conceptual tool subculture, but as soon as we apply the tool to other areas the model breaks down. Indeed, it begins to break down even before that: Maurer is forced to admit that ". . . these subcultures intermingle at many points with the dominant culture, and in some instances—like that of the moonshiner in the agricultural South—are almost indistinguishable from it . . ."[3]

As soon as we turn to subcultures associated with different levels of social class, with different regions of the country, or the like, the big circle-little circles model becomes unworkable. If there is a New England subculture, an Appalachian one, a West Coast subculture, and so on, how are we to locate a national culture? This sort of problem led to an alternative model. Whereas the first assumes that the dominant culture is an entity existing independently of the subcultures within it, the alternative view postulates that the dominant culture is merely the sum of the subcultures which make it up. Using Maurer's imagery, we can again visualize subcultures as very small circles, but now they are over-lapping and clustered in such a way as to approximate the form of a large circle; the dominant culture is then this larger circle, which is no more than the totality of the smaller circles. Milton Gordon, for example, in a discussion which appears as Chapter Thirteen of this volume, speaks of "cultural pluralism" as a term "used to describe the model of American society as a composite of groups which have preserved their own cultural identity." And Thomas Lasswell speaks of "those variant cultural beliefs and behaviors from which the generalization of national culture is drawn."[4]

But this model also over-emphasizes distinctions between sub-cultures, and fails to give an adequate picture of the consistent features of the national culture. The first model, carried far enough, leads one to the position that there is on the one hand a clearly ascertainable national culture, and separate subcultures on the other, and never the twain shall meet. The second model, carried to its logical conclusion, leads to the position that there is no national culture, no consistent strains throughout the society, but only a hodge-podge of subcultures.

How did such a pair of alternatives develop? Answering this question will allow us to break out of the dilemma they present and formulate a more valid model. Both models, as indicated above, resulted from a reification of the concepts "culture" and "subculture." Grouping related norms, etc., into cultures and subcultures is very useful, provided we do not try to push the abstraction too far. These concepts stem from our recognition that any group of people, any society, has collections of individual norms, values, symbols, etc., which more or less hang together and order the activities of the society. We then call such a system a culture (if we are looking at a total society) or a subculture (if we are looking at a sub-unit of the total society), and in so doing are aided by being able to work with larger units of social reality. Problems arise only if we then think that these larger units are all there is to social reality, and thus that their boundaries constitute real borders that cannot be crossed. It was because sociologists frequently lose sight of the smaller units, particularly norms, that models such as the two just presented came into existence.

If we turn back to norms it becomes obvious that some norms extend in basically the same form throughout the entire society, some extend throughout the society but vary somewhat from one part to another, and some norms are held only within certain sub-units of the society.

If we now reconstruct our cultures and subcultures, we arrive at a model that contains both of these, as did the first model, but not in the mutually exclusive manner which that model did. Thus we can have, at one extreme, subcultures sharing almost no elements of the national culture—the Gypsies might be an example of such a subculture—and at the other extreme subcultures having few or no truly unique elements, but only variant patterns—here we might look to regional or class subcultures for examples. And of course all possible combinations could occur between these extremes.

A search of the literature shows that there are a few considerations of subculture that are consistent with this model. For example, Cressey has defined subculture as:

> . . . a set of conduct norms which cluster together in such a way that they can be differentiated from the broader culture of which they are a part. Thus, if some of the rules for behavior in the working class are different from some of the rules for behavior in the middle class, it is proper to speak of a "working-class subculture" and a "middle-class subculture," despite the fact that in these two social classes there are so many identical rules of conduct that it is reasonable to consider the two classes as belonging to the same culture.[5]

This view clearly conforms to the third model, carefully avoiding the traps of the first two. Etzioni has presented a similar view:

> The American Society is not a . . . universal melting pot, into which all ethnic groups "blend" sooner or later, by accepting the dominant culture of the real American tradition. It is, as has often been pointed out, a pluralistic society, with many subcultures and subgroups. All integrated groups accept some values of American society, but at the same time hold their own particularistic tradition and values.[6]

II.

Up to now I have been talking about subcultures, the normative social worlds in which people carry out their day-to-day activities. I have not been talking about the people themselves. I now turn to these members of subcultures.

From the definition of subculture and the model presented above, of subcultures and the total culture, it follows that a person need not live out his life within the boundaries of a single cultural entity. Indeed, in a complex society such as ours it would be rather hard to do so. Were this not the case it would suffice to look only at the total culture, various subcultures, and the relationships between all of these, and not at how concrete individuals fit into this picture. But the fact of multiple involvement in subcultures requires that we attend to the individual level as well.

Virtually every person participates in several subcultures, and he can participate in each of these to different degrees. This variation can occur along lines of time, intensity, and extensiveness. A member may spend only a small portion, a moderate portion, or all his time in a given subculture. Furthermore, while a member can apportion time to various subcultures at different periods, he can also participate in two or more simultaneously. The intensity of participation and attachment also can vary. A person may manifest a high level of affect toward one subculture of which he is a member, but a much lower level toward another to which he also belongs. And he may participate, with whatever expenditure of time and affect, in the entire subculture, or in just part of it. Since "subculture" is the sociologist's way of delineating boundaries around presumed systems of norms, it is reasonable to expect that not all participants will draw the boundaries in the same manner. And even if they do, given the nature of most subcultures, they need not follow all the normative directions of a subculture.

An image of social classes which can be generalized to subcultures of any sort and which might help the reader to visualize the model I have been discussing has been presented by G. D. H. Cole:

> *Classes . . . are not sharply definable groups whose precise numbers can be determined by gathering in enough information about every individual. They are rather aggregations of persons round a number of central nuclei, in such a way that it can be said with confidence of those nearer each centre that they are members of a particular class, but that those further from a centre can be assigned to the class it represents only with increasing uncertainty. Moreover, an individual can be within the sphere of more than one class at the same moment, so that he cannot be assigned wholly to one class; and there exist individuals who can hardly be assigned to any class, even in the most tentative way. It does not follow, because societies have classes within them, that every person attached to them must be assignable to a class.*[7]

Failure to take into account the variable nature of members' affiliations with subcultures has led to the sorts of distortions alluded to in the opening paragraph of this chapter. For example, Cloward and Ohlin, while recognizing the existence of this variability, still argue for ignoring it:

> *At any one point in time, however, the extent to which the norms of the delinquent subculture control behavior will vary from one member to another. Accordingly, descriptions of these subcultures must be stated in terms of the fully indoctrinated member rather than the average member. Only in this way can the distinctiveness of delinquent styles of life be made clear.*[8]

What distinctiveness? One imposed by the conceptual framework of the sociologist? There are real and important differences between subcultures—after all, that is a central reason for looking at them—but their boundaries are more like those between the colors of a rainbow than those between the colors of a Mondrian painting. Cloward and Ohlin are discussing sociological *description,* and for this goal their proposal does have some merit. But if the distinctive features of subcultures are described, to meet the standards of valid sociological research such a description must be followed by a description of the actual looseness of the boundaries which had been sharply drawn only for convenience.

When we pursue the goal of sociological *explanation,* the Cloward and Ohlin approach leads to serious difficulties. Since people live out their lives within subcultures, it is from participation in these subcultures (i.e., from interaction with the other members) that they develop many if not all of their attitudes and patterns of behavior. Thus we turn to subcultures to help explain why segments of the population engage in the different sorts of social action they do. But subcultures overlap one other and the total national culture, and if people can participate in a number of subcultures—either serially or simultaneously—and can participate in each of these in varying degrees, then trying to use all-or-none membership in single subcultures as an explanatory factor can never result in more than partial success.

Rather than treating "subculture" as an isolated concept, then, we should couple it with another concept which focusses our attention on this variant factor of subcultural attachment. Although up to now students of subcultures have not done this, we need not create such a concept out of whole cloth. With only minor modifications, the concept of marginality first developed by Robert Park in 1928 to deal with persons on the boundaries between racial or ethnic groups will give us what we need to avoid over-concretizing the notion of subculture.

In his discussion of marginality, Park defined the marinal man as "a cultural hybrid, a man living and sharing intimately in the cultural life and traditions of two distinct peoples; . . . He was a man on the margin of two cultures and two societies . . ."[9] In another article three years later Park added that:

The typical marginal man is a mixed blood, an Eurasian, mestizo, or mulatto, i.e., a man who by the very fact of his racial origin is predestined to occupy a position somewhere between the two cultures represented by his respective parents.[10]

The concept remained in basically this form until 1940, when Cuber suggested extending its applicability:

The concept of marginality might also be employed to designate persons who occupy a peripheral role between any two differentiated but largely exclusive institutions, culture complexes, or other cultural segments.[11]

This comes much closer to what we need to supplement the subculture concept. An approach similar to Cuber's was taken by Shibutani in 1961, when he suggested that "some men are marginal in that they stand on the border between two or more social worlds but are not accepted as full participants in either."[12]

Whereas Park's treatment of marginality viewed it as being the result of birth, of being born into a position between two cultures, Cuber and Shibutani view it as any situation which involves marginality, whether the person is born into it or not. But in either case one is marginal only by being *between* two or more cultural entities. For our purposes it is necessary that we consider a person as being marginal when on the edge of any subculture, whether this places him automatically on the edge of another subculture or not. Or more precisely, his *relationship* is one of marginality. Since an individual may have any number of marginal attachments to subcultures, it is no longer useful to dichotomize individuals into marginal and non-marginal. Rather, in looking at the impact of a subculture we will distinguish between persons who are marginal to that subculture and those whose relationship to it is non-marginal, that is, who are core members of the subculture. By doing this we have a general concept of subcultural marginality which can be used in any subculture analysis.

Marginality viewed in this manner corresponds to the situation of being a peripheral (rather than core) member of one of Yablonsky's "near-groups," and to being relatively far from the central nucleus of one of Cole's classes.

The reader with some knowledge of statistics might note that coupling "marginality" to "subculture" as suggested here is analogous to coupling "standard deviation" (or more generally, measures of disperson or variability) to "mean" (or more generally, measures of central tendency). Using one alone gives a summary view and describes typicalities, but it oversimplifies. Adding the second concept high-lights the *extent* to which that called "typical" is truly typical. To compare two means we need standard deviation to evaluate overlap: are the two distributions really as disparate as it appears? To compare two subcultures we need marginality for the same reason.

FOOTNOTES

[1]David W. Maurer, *Whiz Mob*, Gainseville, Florida: Publication of the American Dialect Society, No. 24, 1955, 10.

[2]*Ibid.*, 11.

[3]*Ibid.*

[4]Thomas Lasswell, *Class and Stratum*, Boston: Houghton Mifflin, 1965, 211.

[5]Donald R. Cressey, "Differential Association and Delinquent Sub-cultures," paper presented in Helsinki, June, 1965, 5.

[6]Amitai Etzioni, "The Ghetto—A Re-evaluation," *Social Forces* (March, 1959), 260.

[7]G. D. H. Cole, *Studies in Class Structure*, London: Routledge and Kegan Paul, 1955, 1.

[8]Richard A. Cloward and Lloyd E. Ohlin, *Delinquency and Opportunity*, Glencoe, Ill.: The Free Press, 1960, 22.

[9]Robert E. Park, "Human Migration and the Marginal Man," *American Journal of Sociology* (May, 1928), 892.

[10]Robert E. Park, "Personality and Cultural Conflict," *Publication of the American Sociological Society* (May, 1931), 109.

[11]John F. Cuber, "Marginal Church Participants," *Sociology and Social Research* (1940), 58.

[12]Tamotsu Shibutani, *Society and Personality*, Englewood Cliffs: Prentice-Hall, 1961, 275.

Part Three

SUBCULTURE
THEORY

Parts I and II dealt with the conceptualization of subculture, focusing on what subcultures are and what their boundaries and interrelations look like. In Part III we move from conceptualization to explanation. Since sociological explanation is based upon the elaboration of sets of general hypotheses and laws, rather than upon a delineation of particulars (as in historical explanation, for instance), this means turning to subculture theory.

In the first section we saw that as early as 1939 Hollingshead had proposed the hypothesis that "Persons in more or less continuous association evolve behavior traits and cultural mechanisms which are unique to the group and differ in some way from those of other groups and from the larger socio-cultural complex."[1] Hollingshead did not indicate why this is the case, however, nor did he elaborate upon it in any way. Since then a number of other social scientists have made passing mention of subculture theory in works primarily concerned with other matters. As their discussions are too brief to warrant attention in separate chapters, I shall review them here before introducing the three chapters that make up this section.

Some writers see subcultures as emerging in response to a situation or problem. Others see them as the result of interaction. Most frequently the alternative explanation is ignored, but in some cases it is given a secondary place. In one case its importance is explicitly denied.

John Gillen, Oscar Lewis, Herbert Gans, and Irving Spergel all treat subcultures as responses. Gillen, in a 1955 article on regional subcultures in the United States, stated that ". . . any culture is in part a set of customary adaptations to natural environment and resources . . ."[2] In 1961, anthropologist Oscar Lewis proposed that:

Many of the traits of the subculture of poverty can be viewed as attempts at local solutions for problems not met by existing institutions and agencies because the people are not eligible for them, cannot afford them, or are suspicious of them.[3]

Five years later he added that the subculture of poverty:

. . . is both an adaptation and a reaction of the poor to their marginal position in a class-stratified, highly individuated, capitalistic society. It represents an effort to cope with feelings of hopelessness and despair which develop from the realization of the improbability of achieving success in terms of the values and goals of the larger society.[4]

Gans, in 1962, presented a similar view:

The subcultures which I have described are *responses* that people make to the *opportunities* and the *deprivations* that they encounter. More specifically, each subculture is an organized set of related responses that has developed out of people's efforts to cope with the opportunities, incentives, and rewards, as well as the deprivations, prohibitions, and pressures which the natural environment and society—that complex of coexisting and competing subcultures—offer to them.... These responses cannot develop in a vacuum. Over the long range, they can be seen as functions of the resources which a society has available, and of the opportunities which it can offer.[5]

Whereas Gillen was concerned with regional subcultures, and Lewis and Gans with social class subcultures, Spergel's concern was with juvenile delinquent subcultures. Writing in 1966, he defined the delinquent subculture as "the dominant system of beliefs, norms, and values of delinquent groups."[6] He proposed that this subculture "may be regarded as a response to three major sociocultural conditions operating within a neighborhood context: the lower class culture, the youth culture, and the opportunity system."[7] Spergel, whose field is social work, then spelled out the content and influence of each of these in more detail. In his comments on the first two of these he again draws on the response perspective:

In lower income neighborhoods a culture develops in response to a set of common life problems ... the youth culture is a response to the discontinuities of the larger American culture which fails to provide adequate role patterns to bridge the age period between childhood and adulthood.[8]

Tamotsu Shibutani, Samuel E. Wallace, and Everett C. Hughes all emphasize interaction in their approaches to subculture theory. Shibutani, in 1955, argues against response theories:

Variations in outlook arise through differential contact and association; the maintenance of social distance—through segregation, conflict, or simply the reading of different literature—leads to the formation of distinct cultures. Thus, people in different social classes develop different modes of life and outlook, not because of anything inherent in economic position, but because similarity of occupation and limitations set by income level dispose them to certain restricted communication channels. Those in different ethnic groups form their own distinctive cultures because their identifications incline them to interact intimately with each other and to maintain reserve before outsiders.[9]

Wallace, in 1965, while stressing interaction, mentions shared problems and implies that the subculture he is studying is a response to them:

One effect of the self and community imposed isolation [of skid rowers] has been the emergence of skid row subculture. Skid rowers share a similar problem of adjustment to their deviance and are in effective interaction with each other.[10]

Wallace, following Cohen, adds that these are "two prerequisites for the emergence of subcultures."[11]

Hughes, too, focuses upon interaction while bringing in the response aspect. Writing in 1969, he states that:

...for a long time, I have insisted that the sub-culture (although I have not often used that name) is a product of interaction within the group as that interaction is affected by the social and ecological interaction of that group with the larger world, especially those parts of the larger world that touch most closely. The sub-culture of medical students would be inconceivable without the rest of the medical system.[12]

As illustrated by the above review, there have been many brief excursions into the realm of subculture theory. The number of extended visits, unfortunately, has been much smaller. The first sustained attempt to develop a theory of subcultures was in Albert K. Cohen's book, Delinquent Boys, *published in 1955. Although the*

*focus of his book was deviance, when he turned to explanation
Cohen recognized that an understanding of delinquent subcultures
had to rest upon an understanding of subcultures in general. The
result was the formulation which appears as Chapter Eight. The other
two chapters in this section are both published here for the first
time. In Chapter Nine John Irwin presents a set of inter-related
hypotheses developed in the course of his study of the California
surfing subculture. Then in Chapter Ten I present a subculture model
which combines two major types of sociological explanation and
which also takes account of the boundary issue raised in Part II.*

FOOTNOTES

[1] See page 22 of this volume.

[2] John Gillen, "National and Regional Cultural Values in the United States," *Social Forces* (Dec. 1955), 112.

[3] Oscar Lewis, *The Children of Sanchez*, New York: Vintage Books, 1961, xxvii.

[4] Oscar Lewis, *La Vida*, New York: Vintage Books, 1966, xliv.

[5] Herbert J. Gans, *The Urban Villagers*, New York: The Free Press of Glencoe, 1962, 249.

[6] Irving Spergel, *Street Gang Work: Theory and Practice*, Reading, Mass.: Addison-Wesley, 1966, 1.

[7] *Ibid.*, 2.

[8] *Ibid.*

[9] Tamotsu Shibutani, "Reference Groups as Perspectives," *American Journal of Sociology* (May 1955), 565–6.

[10] Samuel E. Wallace, *Skid Row As a Way of Life*, New York: Harper Torchbook, 1965, 149.

[11] *Ibid.* Also see Chapter Eight of this volume, especially page 102.

[12] Everett C. Hughes, in personal communication (typewritten comments on an earlier draft of this volume), April 1969.

8

A GENERAL THEORY
OF SUBCULTURES

Albert K. Cohen

INTRODUCTION

This is a chapter on subcultures in general, how they get started and what keeps them going. This seeming digression is really an integral part of our task. Any explanation of a particular event or phenomenon presupposes an underlying theory, a set of general rules or a model to which all events or phenomena of the same class are supposed to conform. Indeed, do we not mean by "explanation" a demonstration that the thing to be explained can be understood as a special case of the working out of such a set of general rules? For example, when we explain to a child why the rubber safety valve on a pressure cooker pops off when the interior of the cooker reaches a certain critical temperature, we first tell him that there are certain well-established relationships between pressure and temperature (which have been technically formulated in physics as Boyle's Law) and then we show him that the behavior of the valve is exactly what we should expect if the rules which describe those relationships are true. We do no more nor less when we explain the velocity of a falling body, the acquisition of a habit, an increase in the price of some commodity or the growth of a subculture. In every case, if the general theory which we invoke does not "fit" other phenomena of the same class, the explanation is not considered satisfactory. Thus, if *some* changes in the price level seem to be consistent with the "laws of supply and demand" but *other* changes in the price level are not, then the "laws" are considered unsatisfactory and *none* of the changes are explained by reference to these laws.

Therefore, it is appropriate that we set forth explicitly, if somewhat sketchily, the theory about subcultures in general that underlies our attempt to explain the delinquent subculture. If the explanation is sound, then the general theory should provide a key to the understanding of other subcultures as well. If the general theory does not fit other subcultures as well, then the explanation of this particular subculture is thrown into question.

ACTION IS PROBLEM-SOLVING

Our point of departure is the "psychogenic" assumption that all human action—not delinquency alone—is an on-going series of efforts to solve problems. By "problems" we do not only mean the worries and dilemmas that bring people to the psychiatrist and the psychological clinic. Whether or not to accept a proffered drink, which of two ties to buy, what to do about the unexpected guest or the "F" in algebra are problems too. They all involve, until they are resolved, a certain tension, a disequilibrium and a challenge. We hover between doing and not doing, doing this or doing that, doing it one way or doing it another. Each choice is an act, each act is a choice. Not every act is a *successful* solution, for our choice may leave us with unresolved tensions or generate new and unanticipated consequences which pose new problems, but it is at least an attempt at a solution. On the other hand, not every problem need imply distress, anxiety, bedevilment. Most problems are familiar and recurrent and we have at hand for them ready solutions, habitual modes of action which we have found efficacious and acceptable both to ourselves and to our neighbors. Other problems, however, are not so readily resolved. They persist, they nag, and they press for novel solutions.

What people do depends upon the problems they contend with. If we want to explain what people do, then we want to be clear about the nature of human problems and what produces them. As a first step, it is important to recognize that all the multifarious factors and circumstances that conspire to produce a problem come from one or the other of two sources, the actor's "frame of reference" and the "situation" he confronts. All problems arise and all problems are solved through changes in one or both of these classes of determinants.

First, the situation. This is the world we live in and where we are located in that world. It includes the physical setting within which we must operate, a finite supply of time and energy with which to accomplish our ends, and above all the habits, the expectations, the demands and the social organization of the people around us. Always our problems are what they are because the situation limits the things we can do and have and the conditions under which they are possible. . . .

But the niggardliness, the crabbiness, the inflexibility of the situation and the problems they imply are always relative to the actor. What the actor sees and how he feels about what he sees depend as much on his "point of view" as on the situation which he encounters. Americans do not see grasshoppers as belonging to the same category as pork chops, orange juice and cereal; other peoples do. Different Americans, confronting a "communist" or a "Negro," have very different ideas of what kind of person they are dealing with. The political office which one man sees as a job, another sees as an opportunity for public service and still another as something onerous and profitless to be avoided at all costs. Our beliefs about what is, what is possible and what consequences flow from what actions do not necessarily correspond to what is "objectively" true. "The facts" never simply stare us in the face. We see them always through a glass, and the glass consists of the interests, preconceptions, stereotypes and values we bring to the situation. This glass is our frame of reference. . . .

Our really hard problems are those for which we have no ready-at-hand solutions which will not leave us without feelings of tension, frustration, resentment, guilt, bitterness, anxiety or hopelessness. These feelings and therefore the inadequacy of the solutions are largely the result of the frame of reference through which we contemplate these solutions. It follows that an effective, really satisfying solution *must entail some change in that frame of reference itself.* The actor may give up pursuit of some goal which seems unattainable, but it is not a "solution" unless he can first persuade himself that the goal is, after all, not worth pursuing; in short, his values must change. He may resolve a problem of conflicting loyalties by persuading himself that the greater obligation attaches to one rather than to the other, but this too involves a change in his frame of reference: a commitment to some standard for adjudicating the claims of different loyalties. "Failure" can be transformed into something less humiliating by imputing to others fraud, malevolence or corruption, but this means adopting new perspectives for looking at others and oneself. He may continue to strive for goals hitherto unattainable by adopting more efficacious but "illicit" means; but, again, the solution is satisfying only to the degree that guilt is obviated by a change in moral standards. All these and other devices are familiar to us as the psychologist's and the psychoanalyst's "mechanisms of adjustment"—projection, rationalization, substitution, etc.—and they are all ways of coping with problems by a change within the actor's frame of reference.

A second factor we must recognize in building up a theory of subcultures is that human problems are not distributed in a random way among the roles that make up a social system. Each age, sex, racial and ethnic category, each occupation, economic stratum and social class consists of people who have been equipped by their society with frames of reference and confronted by their society with situations which are not equally characteristic of other roles. If the ingredients of which problems are compounded are likened to a deck of cards, your chances and mine of getting a certain hand are not the same but are strongly affected by where we happen to sit. The problems and preoccupations of men and women are different because they judge themselves and others judge them by different standards and because the means available to them for realizing their aspirations are different. It is obvious that opportunities for the achievement of power and prestige are not the same for people who start out at different positions in the class system; it is perhaps a bit less obvious that their levels of aspiration in these respects and therefore what it will take to satisfy them are likely also to differ. All of us must come to terms with the problems of growing old, but these problems are not the same for all of us. To consider but one facet, the decline of physical vigor may have very different meaning for a steel worker and a physician. There is a large and increasing scholarly literature, psychiatric and sociological, on the ways in which the structure of society generates, at each position within the system, characteristic combinations of personality and situation and therefore characteristic problems of adjustment.

Neither sociologists nor psychiatrists, however, have been sufficiently diligent in exploring the role of the social structure and the immediate social milieu in determining *the creation and selection of solutions*. A way of acting is never completely explained by describing, however convincingly, the problems of adjustment to which it is a response, *as long as there are conceivable alternative responses*. Different individuals *do* deal differently with the same or similar problems and these differences must likewise be accounted for. One man responds to a barrier on the route to his goal by redoubling his efforts. Another seeks for a more devious route to the same objective. Another succeeds in convincing himself that the game is not worth the candle. Still another accepts, but with ill grace and an abiding feeling of bitterness and frustration, the inevitability of failure. Here we shall explore some of the ways in which the fact that we are participants in a system of social interaction affects the ways in which we deal with our problems.

PRESSURES TOWARD CONFORMITY

In a general way it is obvious that any solution that runs counter to the strong interests or moral sentiments of those around us invites punishment or the forfeiture of satisfactions which may be more distressing than the problem with which it was designed to cope. We seek, if possible, solutions which will settle old problems and not create new ones. A first requirement, then, of a wholly acceptable solution is that it be acceptable to those on whose cooperation and good will we are dependent. This immediately imposes sharp limits on the range of creativity and innovation. Our dependence upon our social milieu provides us with a strong incentive to select our solutions from among those already established and known to be congenial to our fellows. . . .

Both on the levels of overt action and of the supporting frame of reference, there are powerful incentives not to deviate from the ways established in our groups. Should our problems be not capable of solution in ways acceptable to our groups and should they be sufficiently pressing, we are not so likely to strike out on our own as we are to shop around for a group with a different subculture, with a frame of reference we find more congenial. One fascinating aspect of the social process is the continual realignment of groups, the migration of individuals from one group to another in the unconscious quest for a social milieu favorable to the resolution of their problems of adjustment.

HOW SUBCULTURAL SOLUTIONS ARISE

Now we confront a dilemma and a paradox. We have seen how difficult it is for the individual to cut loose from the culture models in his milieu, how his dependence upon his fellows compels him to seek conformity and to avoid innovation. But these models and precedents which we call the surrounding culture are ways in which other people think and other people act, and these other people are likewise constrained by models in *their* milieux. *These models themselves, however, continually change.* How is it possible for cultural innovations to emerge while each of the participants in the culture is so powerfully motivated to conform to what is already established? This is the central theoretical problem of this book.

The crucial condition for the emergence of new cultural forms is the existence, *in effective interaction with one another, of a number of actors with similar problems of adjustment.* These may be the entire membership of a group or only certain members, similarly circumstanced, within the group. Among the conceivable solutions to their problems may be one which is not yet embodied in action and which does not therefore exist as a cultural model. This solution, except for the fact that it does not already carry the social criteria of validity and promise the social rewards of consensus, might well answer more neatly to the problems of this group and appeal to its members more effectively than any of the solutions already institutionalized. For each participant, this solution would be adjustive and adequately motivated provided that he could anticipate a simultaneous and corresponding transformation in the frames of reference of his fellows. Each would welcome a sign from the others that a new departure in this direction would receive approval and support. But how does one *know* whether a gesture toward innovation will strike a responsive and sympathetic chord in others or whether it will elicit hostility, ridicule and punishment? *Potential* concurrence is always problematical and innovation or the impulse to innovate a stimulus for anxiety.

The paradox is resolved when the innovation is broached in such a manner as to elicit from others reactions suggesting their receptivity; and when, at the same time, the innovation occurs by increments so small, tentative and ambiguous as to permit the actor to retreat, if the signs be unfavorable, without having become identified with an unpopular position. Perhaps all social actions have, in addition to their instrumental, communicative and expressive functions, this quality of being *exploratory gestures.* For the actor with problems of adjustment which cannot be resolved within the frame of reference of the established culture, each response of the other to what the actor says and does is a clue to the directions in which change may proceed further in a way congenial to the other and to the direction in which change will lack social support. And if the probing gesture is motivated by tensions common to other participants it is likely to initiate a process of *mutual* exploration and *joint* elaboration of a new solution. My exploratory gesture functions as a cue to you; your exploratory gesture as a cue to me. By a casual, semi-serious, noncommital or tangential remark I may stick my neck out just a little way, but I will quickly withdraw it unless you, by some sign of affirmation, stick *yours* out. I will permit myself to become progressively committed but only as others, by some visible sign, become likewise committed. The final product, to which we are jointly committed, is likely to be a compromise formation of all the participants to what we may call a cultural process, a formation perhaps unanticipated by any of them. Each actor may contribute something directly to the growing product, but he may also contribute indirectly by encouraging others to advance, inducing them to retreat, and suggesting new avenues to be explored. The product cannot be ascribed to any one of the participants; it is a real "emergent" on a group level.

We may think of this process as one of mutual conversion. The important thing to remember is that we do not first convert ourselves and then others. The acceptability of an idea to oneself depends upon its acceptability to others. Converting the other is part of the process of converting oneself. . . .

The late Kurt Lewin, on the basis of his experience in attempts at guided social change, remarks:

> . . . *Experience in leadership training, in changing of food habits, work production, criminality, alcoholism, prejudices, all seem to indicate that it is usually easier to change individuals formed into a group than to change any one of them separately. As long as group values are unchanged the individual will resist changes more strongly the farther he is to depart from group standards. If the group standard itself is changed, the resistance which is due to the relationship between individual and group standard is eliminated.*[1]

The emergence of these "group standards" of this shared frame of reference, is the emergence of a new subculture. It is cultural because each actor's participation in this system of norms is influenced by his perception of the same norms in other actors. It is *sub*cultural because the norms are shared only among those actors who stand somehow to profit from them and who find in one another a sympathetic moral climate within which these norms may come to fruition and persist. In this fashion culture is continually being created, re-created and modified wherever individuals sense in one another like needs, generated by like circumstances, not shared generally in the larger social system. Once established, such a subcultural system may persist, but not by sheer inertia. It may achieve a life which outlasts that of the individuals who participated in its creation, but only so long as it continues to serve the needs of those who succeed its creators.

SUBCULTURAL SOLUTIONS TO STATUS PROBLEMS

One variant of this cultural process interests us especially because it provides the model for our explanation of the delinquent subculture. Status problems are problems of achieving respect in the eyes of one's fellows. Our ability to achieve status depends upon the criteria of status applied by our fellows, that is, the standards or norms they go by in evaluating people. These criteria are an aspect of their cultural frames of reference. If we lack the characteristics or capacities which give status in terms of these criteria, we are beset by one of the most typical and yet distressing of human problems of adjustment. One solution is for individuals who share such problems to gravitate toward one another and jointly to establish new norms, new criteria of status which define as meritorious the characteristics they *do* posses, the kinds of conduct of which they *are* capable. It is clearly necessary for each participant, if the innovation is to solve his status problem, that these new criteria be shared with others, that the solution be a group and not a private solution. If he "goes it alone" he succeeds only in further estranging himself from his fellows. Such new status criteria would represent new subcultural values different from or even antithetical to those of the larger social system. . . .

SOME ACCOMPANIMENTS OF THE
CULTURAL PROCESS

The continued serviceability and therefore the viability of a subcultural solution entails the emergence of a certain amount of group solidarity and heightened interaction among the participants in the subculture. It is only in interaction with those who share his values that the actor finds social validation for his beliefs and social rewards for his way of life, and the continued existence of the group and friendly intercourse with its members become values for actor. Furthermore, to the extent that the new subculture invites the hostility of outsiders—one of the costs of subcultural solutions—the members of the subcultural group are motivated to look to one another for those goods and services, those relationships of cooperation and exchange which they once enjoyed with the world outside the group and which have now been withdrawn. This accentuates still further the separateness of the group, the dependence of the members on the group and the richness and individuality of its subculture. No group, of course, can live entirely unto itself. To some extent the group may be compelled to improvise new arrangements for obtaining services from the outside world. "The fix," for example, arises to provide for the underworld that protection which is afforded to legitimate business by the formal legal system and insurance companies.

Insofar as the new subculture represents a new status system sanctioning behavior tabooed or frowned upon by the larger society, the acquisition of status within the new group is accompanied by a loss of status outside the group. To the extent that the esteem of outsiders is a value to the members of the group, a new problem is engendered. To this problem the typical solution is to devalue the good will and respect of those whose good will and respect are forfeit anyway. The new subculture of the community of innovators comes to include hostile and contemptuous images of those groups whose enmity they have earned. Indeed, this repudiation of outsiders, necessary in order to protect oneself from feeling concerned about what they may think, may go so far as to make nonconformity with the expectations of the outsiders a positive criterion of status within the group. Certain kinds of conduct, that is, become reputable precisely because they are disreputable in the eyes of the "out-group." . . .

CONCLUSION

Our point of departure, we have said, is the psychogenic assumption that innovations, whether on the level of action or of the underlying frame of reference, arise out of problems of adjustment. In the psychogenic model, however, the innovation is independently contrived by the actor. The role of the social milieu in the genesis of the problem is recognized, but its role in the determination of the solution minimized. In the psychogenic model, the fact that others have problems similar to my own may lead them to contrive like solutions, but my problem-solving process runs to its conclusion unaffected by the parallel problem-solving processes of the others.

In the pure or extreme cultural-transmission model, on the other hand, the role of important differences in problems of adjustment and the motivation of newly acquired behavior by those problems tend to drop out of sight. Above all, the pure cultural-transmission view fails completely to explain the origin of new cultural patterns. Indeed, if the view we have proposed is correct, the cultural-transmission model fails to explain even the perpetuation of a cultural pattern through social transmission, for the recruitment of new culture-bearers presupposes life-problems which render them susceptible to the established pattern. The theory we have outlined, couched in terms of group problem-solving, attempts to integrate two views which, in the literature, frequently stand in presumed contrast to one another.

It is to be emphasized that the existence of problems of adjustment, even of like problems of adjustment among a plurality of actors, is not sufficient to insure the emergence of a subcultural solution. The existence of the necessary conditions for effective social interaction prerequisite to such a solution cannot be taken for granted. Who associates with whom is partly a matter of "shopping around" and finding kindred souls. But circumstances may limit this process of mutual gravitation of people with like problems and free and spontaneous communication among them. People with like problems may be so separated by barriers of physical space or social convention that the probability of mutual exploration and discovery is small. Free choice of associates may be regulated by persons in power, as parents may regulate the associates of their children. Where status differences among people with like problems are great, the probability of spontaneous communication relating to private, intimate, emotionally involved matters is small. Where the problems themselves are of a peculiarly delicate, guilt-laden nature, like many problems arising in the area of sex, inhibitions on communication may be so powerful that persons with like problems may never reveal themselves to one another, although circumstances are otherwise favorable for mutual exploration. Or the problems themselves may be so infrequent and atypical that the probability of running into someone else whose interests would be served by a common solution is negligible.

Because of all these restraints and barriers to communication, as well as the costs of participation in subcultural groups, which may sometimes be counted excessive, subcultural solutions may not emerge, or particular individuals may not participate in them. Nonetheless, the problems of adjustment may be sufficiently intense and persistent that they still press for some kind of change that will mitigate or resolve the problem. Since group solutions are precluded, the problem-solving may well take a "private," "personal-social" or "neurotic" direction and be capable of satisfactory description in primarily psychogenic terms.

A complete theory of subcultural differentiation would state more precisely the conditions under which subcultures emerge and fail to emerge, and would state operations for predicting the content of subcultural solutions. Such a task is beyond the scope of this chapter, and, in any case, the completion of this theory must await a great deal more of hard thinking and research. In this chapter we have tried to put on the record, in a highly general and schematic way, the basic theoretical assumptions which underlie the chapters which are to follow. In these chapters, in conformity with the model we have proposed, we shall try to demonstrate that certain problems of adjustment tend, in consequence of the structure of American society, to occur most typically in those role sectors where the delinquent subculture is endemic. Then we shall try to show how the delinquent subculture provides a solution appropriate to those particular problems and to elaboration and perpetuation by social groups.

FOOTNOTE

[1]Kurt Lewin, "Frontiers of Group Dynamics," *Human Relations,* (June, 1947), 35.

9

DEVIANT BEHAVIOR AS A SUBCULTURAL PHENOMENON

John Irwin

In this report the surfers of Southern California were used to trace the development of a deviant subculture, to emphasize several points of importance in the analysis of deviant behavior as a subcultural phenomenon and to formulate certain necessary conditions that must be present for the formation and perpetuation of a new subculture. With regard to the above purposes, the following specific points were stressed:

1. Systematic deviant behavior carried on by groups has no meaning outside its subcultural context. To try to understand it in terms of the beliefs, values and attitudes of the greater society is

From John Irwin, *Surfers: A Study of the Growth of a Deviant Subculture*, unpublished thesis, University of California, Berkeley, 1965.

fruitless. Any attempt to point to causes of this form of deviant behavior must begin with an understanding of the behavior in its setting of values, beliefs and symbolic systems of the perpetuators of the particular behavior. . . .

2. A subculture is formed when a group of persons remains in interaction or communication over an extended period of time and experiences a re-organization of their beliefs, values and symbolic systems around the particular circumstances of their common relationships. The following conditions have been offered as those which are necessary for this re-organization to occur:

a. The group must be allowed to continue in interaction over a protracted *time* period.

b. Aside from the external liberty to continue as a group, there must be a strong *commitment* to the group.

c. There must be a certain degree of general *congruence* of the individual members' values and beliefs. It is especially important that there is no high degree of conflict between the orientation systems of the individuals.

d. There must be *distinct qualities* in the activities or interests of the group.

Another condition must be present to permit a subculture to develop aspects which are in violation of the standards of the conventional society:

e. The membership of the groups developing the subculture cannot have a strong commitment to conventional values and beliefs.

f. Finally, there is a necessary condition for the perpetuation of a subculture. It was seen in the case of the surfing subculture that its inability to fulfill this condition led to its almost complete demise. The means of controlling external relations of the group must be available or feasible. This condition has two parts. The first, in case of approval by outsiders to the group, means to control the influx of new members must exist. The second is in case of disapproval by outsiders. This ranges from means to cope with the invocation of informal sanctions, to ways of handling direct formal attempts to sanction and/or destroy the group through such means as incarceration.

3. In conclusion, a subculture must be analyzed historically. With the concept of subculture that was presented here—as something strongly akin to the concept "culture" which is changing and evolving constantly—to understand the behavior of the subculture participants, the investigator must be cognizant of the time dimension of the phenomenon. Subcultural systems are undergoing constant changes due to internal processes of growth and change, and due to varying circumstances of the greater cultural-social setting of the subculture. Therefore, certain behavior at one point of time does not have the same meaning, and relationship to the subculture as it has at another time. All considerations of cause must be made with this relationship in mind.

10

A PROCESS MODEL
OF SUBCULTURES

David O. Arnold

Most of the research on subcultures had had a descriptive goal: the concept of subculture, however defined, is used to mark off an area of the social world which is then described by the researcher. But sociology seeks to explain as well as to describe. Therefore, in this chapter I present a theoretical model which treats subcultures in an explanatory fashion, both to account for their development and change and to explain their effects on the individuals who are affiliated with them.

First, however, it is necessary to consider the sorts of explanations which sociologists have attempted in this area. In his article on behavior systems (which appears as Chapter Two of this volume) Hollingshead suggests that "analysis of behavior systems should be concentrated on three problems: the definition of the system; its life

Prepared for this volume.

history; and its relation to the larger society." The first and last of these are primarily descriptive questions; problems of explanation are brought up by the second, which Hollingshead defines as being "oriented around the question as to how a system comes into existence, is maintained from generation to generation, and perhaps passes away." To make this more complete I would also ask how changes, if any, come about. These issues take the subcultural system alone as the unit of analysis. Another area in which the goal of explanation can be pursued would relate the subculture to the individuals who guide their actions by it: who adopts the subculture, why and how do they do so, and what effect does this adoption have on these individuals?

Three main approaches to explanation are used in sociology today: the functional, the structural, and the interactionist. The first of these, while useful for many purposes, cannot help answer the questions I have raised regarding subcultures. This leaves the structural and the interactionist as possible ways of dealing with them. Up to now there has been an assumed opposition between these, with structural sociologists tending to ignore the interactionist approach and interactionists actively arguing against the structural. Each presents a convincing picture of the incompleteness of the other. Starting with interaction constitutes jumping into the middle of the problem: granted that interaction can account for attitudes, beliefs, behavior, etc., why does the interaction occur in the manner it does? For example, Sutherland's hypothesis that criminal patterns are adopted when a person's interaction with holders of criminal patterns is greater than his interaction with holders of anti-criminal patterns[1], begs the question of why the person has this greater interaction in the first place. On the other hand, to say that structural position (e.g., high socioeconomic status) "causes" a given attitude or behavior (e.g., voting Republican) assumes some almost mystical connection between independent and dependent variables, and substitutes correlation for a thorough deliniation of the causal process.

Whereas functionalists have realized that the most fruitful application of their frame of reference occurs when combined with the structural in a structural-functional format, no similar *rapprochement* has developed between structuralists and interactionists. Yet by combining these two we can avoid the gaps that the use of either one independently builds into our attempts at explanation. Structure might better be viewed as facilitating and setting limits upon interaction, and interaction as leading to various attitudinal and behavioral outcomes. Thus in a sense what is involved is using structure as an independent variable and interaction as an intervening variable. In this way we need neither stop with bare structural description (or with an assumption of causation), nor assume the unexplained existence of interaction.

I.

Much of the work in this field has left unclear whether subculture refers to a group of people or to the shared ideas of a group of people. In examining and working with the structural-interactionist subculture model it is important to view subcultures as systems of norms, not as groups of concrete individuals. The model looks at the people involved in order to explain how the subculture develops. While subcultures grow out of the interaction of groups of people, they are not themselves those groups, nor are the participants in any given subculture exactly the same as the membership of the segment from which it arose. This distinction must be maintained since the extent to which the two are related is an important empirical problem, and can only be investigated if the empirical relationship between them is left problematic by the research model.

The first element of the structural-interactionist model is structural position, that is, specification and description of the population segment under consideration. The second element is differential interaction: persons belonging to the same population segment tend to interact more with each other than with persons belonging to other segments. There are both positive and negative reasons for this, the positive encouraging intra-segmental interaction, and the negative discouraging inter-segmental interaction. The precise content of these would vary with the particular structural dimension being considered, but on the positive side could include similar problems, propinquity, similar resources, etc., and on the negative side the reverse of these.

The third element of the model is the segment-related subculture, that is, the subculture that results from the differential interaction of people sharing the same structural position. Although interaction can be thought of as directly influencing the individual, this seems only rarely to hold true. Each time individuals interact they do not do so with a clean slate such that they find it necessary to create unique solutions to each problem confronting them. Rather, over time an interrelated set of shared understandings, a system of norms, a subculture, develops out of repeated interaction. Once this occurs further interaction serves to transmit this subculture in routine situations, and to draw upon it in handling non-routine situations. In the latter case this also results in the subculture itself being modified.

Finally, as the fourth element—actually elements—we have the individual manifestations of subcultural membership, i.e., individual variations in behavior, attitudes, beliefs, etc.

The model can now be laid out pictorially in the following manner:

structural position ⟶ differential interaction ⟶ segment-related subculture ⟶ individual attitudes, behavior, etc.

Actually social behavior does not exhibit such a one-way pattern of development. In addition to a causal arrow connecting each element with the next, there must be certain arrows running from the later elements to the earlier ones. Some such reverse arrows would apply only for certain kinds of structural differentiations and resultant subcultures, and not for others, and thus cannot be inserted here in the general model. In applying this model on any more concrete level, however, it should be remembered that as presented above the model is a simplification of the actual causal process.

Many of the supposed attempts to explain subcultures have actually been attempts to explain the attitudes and behavior of individuals who adopt these subcultures. One reason for this confusion is that the two sorts of problems are not independent. The same process that accounts for the development of a subculture which previously did not exist may also account for the affiliation of individuals with one that is in existence.

Applying the model to the explanation of subcultures *per se*, we should find that individuals sharing similar statuses interact more with each other than would be expected by chance, and that out of this interaction comes a system of beliefs, values, and norms—i.e., a subculture—which is at least somewhat unique, and which can be traced to the particular problems and facilities presented by the shared statuses and to the relative separation or isolation from persons occupying different statuses. Applying the model to individuals, where a relevant subculture is already in existence, we should find that a similar interaction takes place and that through this interaction new occupants of the relevant statuses are socialized into the subculture and thus begin to think and act in accord with its prescriptions. Note that on the individual level all elements of the model come into play, whereas on the aggregate or cultural level only the first three do.

II.

So far the model has been presented in ideal form, and thus oversimplifies the process as it occurs in the empirical world. As such it implies a much stronger determinism resulting from particular structural positions than can actually be demonstrated. If there were clean breaks between subcultures, with all persons being firmly attached to one or another of them, the model might be adequate as it stands. But such is not the case. Rather, many people have at best what might be considered marginal attachment to certain subcultures (See Chapter Seven, "Subculture Marginality"), requiring modification in the operation of the model.

If an individual is clearly positioned within a particular structural population segment this will exert a strong influence on his interaction, which therefore will be very differential (i.e., the ratio of within-segment to between-segment interaction will be high), resulting in strong attachment to the subcultural system. If, by contrast, an individual's structural location is marginal to some particular segment (or pair of segments, or indeed to the dimension along which the segments are arrayed), his interaction will be less determined, and accordingly his attachment to a particular subculture will be weaker. Because of this such a person's actions, attitudes, and so forth, will exhibit more variation (from the conventional patterns of the subculture) than those of the non-marginal person. Such an outcome is consistent with Park's conception of marginality as freeing people from the determinism of a single group[2], and with Shibutani's statement that:

> *People who occupy a marginal status are continually confronted*
> *with the necessity of forming moral judgments. Situations that*
> *would be routine for other people call for choice...*[3]

The effect of marginality on the operation of the model can be seen at the aggregate as well as the individual level. First, considering subculture formation, the less the average structural marginality, *vis-a-vis* a particular status, of the occupants of that status, the more cohesive and differentiated from other subcultures will be the subculture stemming from that status. Conversely, the greater the average structural marginality, the more diffuse the boundaries of the resultant subculture. Thus the nature of any subculture is dependent not only upon the nature of the structural position from which it develops, but also upon the amount of marginality typically manifested in regard to that position. As always, additional factors not considered here may also be operating.

Second, considering subcultures already in existence, if we divide persons belonging to any given structural segment into those whose membership is marginal and those whose membership is non-marginal, we should find much greater attitudinal and behavioral heterogeneity among the marginal members. Thus the model can also aid in predicting and explaining conformity and non-conformity to subcultural standards.

FOOTNOTES

[1] Edwin H. Sutherland, and Donald R. Cressey, *Principles of Criminology*, seventh edition, Philadelphia: Lippincott, 1966, Chapter 4.

[2] Robert E. Park, "Introduction" to Everett V. Stonequist, *The Marginal Man*, New York: Russell & Russell, 1961 (first published in 1937 by Charles Scribner's Sons), xvii–xviii; also "The Nature of Race Relations," in *Race Relations and the Race Problem*, Edgar T. Thompson, ed., Durham: Duke University Press, 1939, 39.

[3] Tamotsu Shibutani, *Society and Personality*, Englewood Cliffs: Prentice-Hall, 1961, 578. The linkage between these notions regarding margin-

ality and Lazarsfeld's notion of "cross-pressures" now becomes apparent. (Paul F. Lazarsfeld, Bernard Berelson, and Hazel Gaudet, *The People's Choice,* New York: Columbia University Press, 1948.) Just as the individual who is tied to two or more different population segments is marginal to the normative systems stemming from each one of them, so the individual tied to differing individuals or having disparate social and personal loyalties is under cross-pressures, and is also torn between two sets of expectations. For the most part, hypotheses developed in working with one of these concepts can be readily translated for application to the other.

Part Four

RECENT
FORMULATIONS

In the final section we return to the topic of Part I: what is a subculture? But whereas in Part I we looked at some seeds, in Part IV we will see saplings; in this field, trees remain to the future. Both Yinger, in Chapter Eleven, and Wolfgang and Ferracuti, in Chapter Twelve, start by building on previous writings, reconceptualizing subculture with the aid of concepts culled from psychology. Despite their commonality, however, they develop very different formulations.

In Chapters Thirteen and Fourteen we conclude with two sociologists who had written earlier on subculture and who have revised their formulations. In Milton Gordon's 1947 article, which appears as Chapter Three of this book, he defined subculture as a sub-division of a national culture based on five elements, one of which is ethnic background. Seventeen years later Gordon expanded his consideration of ethnicity with the publication of his book Assimilation in American Life. *In it he presents the view of subculture reprinted here in Chapter Thirteen. This time he places subculture in a more formal context, distinguishing between social structure and culture, dividing these into three levels, then identifying subculture within this framework. Although Gordon's focus here is primarily on ethnic subcultures and on what he terms the "ethclass," the broader applicability of what he says is as clear as that of the writers who focused on delinquent subcultures.*

Finally, in Chapter Fourteen, Irwin opens up a new issue by suggesting that our ways of viewing subcultures must change because the nature of subcultures themselves has been changing. Whereas the concept subculture was once used only by the sociologist to organize his understanding of the social world, it is now used by the very members of that social world to organize their activity within it.

11

CONTRACULTURE
AND SUBCULTURE

J. Milton Yinger

In recent years there has been widespread and fruitful employment of the concept of subculture in sociological and anthropological research. The term has been used to focus attention not only on the wide diversity of norms to be found in many societies but on the normative aspects of deviant behavior. The ease with which the term has been adopted, with little study of its exact meaning or its values and its difficulties, is indicative of its utility in emphasizing a sociological point of view in research that has been strongly influenced both by individualistic and moralistic interpretations. To describe the normative qualities of an occupation, to contrast the value systems of social classes, or to emphasize the controlling power of the code of a delinquent gang is to underline a sociological aspect

Reprinted with permission of author and publisher from *American Sociological Review*, Volume 25, October 1960, pp. 625-635.

of these phenomena that is often disregarded.

In the early days of sociology and anthropology, a key task was to document the enormous variability of culture from society to society and to explore the significance of the overly simplified but useful idea that "the mores can make anything right." In recent years that task has been extended to the study of the enormous variability of culture *within* some societies. It is unfortunate that "subculture," a central concept in this process, has seldom been adequately defined.[1] It has been used as an *ad hoc* concept whenever a writer wished to emphasize the normative aspects of behavior that differed from some general standard. The result has been a blurring of the meaning of the term, confusion with other terms, and a failure frequently to distinguish between two levels of social causation.

THREE USAGES OF SUBCULTURE

Few concepts appear so often in current sociological writing. In the course of twelve months, I have noted over 100 books and articles that make some use, from incidental to elaborate, of the idea of "subculture." The usages vary so widely, however, that the value of the term is severely limited. If chemists had only one word to refer to all colorless liquids and this led them to pay attention to only the two characteristics shared in common, their analysis would be exceedingly primitive. Such an analogy overstates the diversity of ideas covered by "subculture," but the range is very wide. Nevertheless three distinct meanings can be described.

In some anthropological work, subculture refers to certain universal tendencies that seem to occur in all societies. They underlie culture, precede it, and set limits to the range of its variation. Thus Kroeber writes: "Indeed, such more or less recurrent near-regularities of form or process as have to date been formulated for culture are actually subcultural in nature. They are limits set to culture by physical or organic factors."[2] In *The Study of Man,* Linton uses subculture to refer to various pan-human phenomena that seem to occur everywhere. Thus good-natured and tyrannical parents may be found in societies that differ widely in their family patterns.[3] This use shades off into other concepts that are similar but not identical: Edward Sapir's "precultural" and Cooley's "human nature" refer to biological and social influences that underlie all cultures.[4] Since subculture is only rarely used today to refer to this series of ideas, I shall exclude them from further consideration, with the suggestion that the use of Sapir's term "precultural" might well clarify our thinking.

Two other usages of subculture represent a much more serious confusion. The term is often used to point to the normative systems of groups smaller than a society, to give emphasis to the ways these groups differ in such things as language, values, religion, diet, and style of life from the larger society of which they are a part. Perhaps the most common referent in this usage is an ethnic enclave (French Canadians in Maine) or a region (the subculture of the South), but the distinctive norms of much smaller and more temporary groups (even a particular friendship group) may be described as a subculture. Kluckhohn, for example, refers to "the subculture of anthropologists" and Riesman to "subcultures among the faculty."

This second meaning, which itself contains some ambiguities, as we shall see, must be distinguished from a third meaning associated with it when the reference is to norms that arise specifically from a frustrating situation or from conflict between a group and the larger society. Thus the emergent norms of a delinquent gang or the standards of an adolescent peer group have often been designated "subcultural." In addition to a cultural dimension, this third usage introduces a social-psychological dimension, for there is direct reference to the personality factors involved in the development and maintenance of the norms. Specifically, such personality tendencies as frustration, anxiety, feelings of role ambiguity, and resentment are shown to be involved in the creation of the subculture. The mutual influence of personality and culture is not a distinctive characteristic of this type of subculture, of course, for they are everywhere interactive. . . .

Yet the nature of the relation is not the same in all cases. The term subculture, when used in the third way described here, raises to a position of prominence one particular kind of dynamic linkage between norms and personality: the creation of a series of inverse or counter values (opposed to those of the surrounding society) in face of serious frustration or conflict. To call attention to the special aspects of this kind of normative system, I suggest the term *contraculture*. Before exploring the relationship between subculture and contraculture, however, the range of meanings given subculture even when it is limited to the second usage requires comment.

SUBCULTURE AND ROLE

The variety of referents for the term subculture is very wide because the normative systems of sub-societies can be differentiated on many grounds. The groups involved may range from a large regional subdivision to a religious sect with only one small congregation. The distinctive norms may involve many aspects of life—religion, language, diet, moral values—or, for example, only a few separate practices among the members of an occupational group. Further distinctions among subcultures might be made on the basis of time (has the subculture persisted through a number of generations?), origin (by migration, absorption by a dominant society, social or physical segregation, occupational specialization, and other sources), and by the mode of relationship to the surrounding culture (from indifference to conflict). Such wide variation in the phenomena covered by a term can be handled by careful specification of the several grounds for subclassification. Confusion has arisen not so much from the scope of the term subculture as from its use as a substitute for "role." Only with great effort is some degree of clarity being achieved in the use of the role concept and the related terms "position" and "role behavior." Were this development retarded by confusion of role with subculture it would be unfortunate. All societies have differentiating roles, but only heterogeneous societies have subcultures. Role is *that part of* a full culture that is assigned, as the appropriate rights and duties, to those occupying a given position.[5] These rights and duties usually interlock into a system with those of persons who occupy other positions. They are known to and accepted by all those who share the culture. Thus the role of a physician is known, at least in vague outline, by most persons in a society and it is seen as part of the total culture. (This is not to prejudge the question of role consensus, for there may be many non-role aspects of being a physician.) But subculture is not tied in this way into the larger cultural complex: it refers to norms that set a group apart from, not those that integrate a group with, the total society. Subcultural norms, as contrasted with role norms, are unknown to, looked down upon, or thought of as separating forces by the other members of a society. There are doubtless subcultural aspects of being a physician—normative influences affecting his behavior that are not part of his role, not culturally designated rights and duties. But the empirical mixture should not obscure the need for this analytic distinction.

Along with confusion with the role concept, subculture carries many of the ambiguities associated with the parent concept of culture. In much social scientific writing it is not at all clear whether culture refers to norms, that is, to expected or valued behavior, or to behavior that is widely followed and therefore normal in a statistical sense only. This dual referent is particularly likely to be found in the work of anthropologists. Perhaps because their concepts are derived largely from the study of relatively more stable and homogeneous societies, they draw less sharply the distinction between the statistically normal and the normative. Sociologists are more apt to find it necessary to explore the tensions between the social order and culture, to be alert to deviations, and they are therefore more likely to define culture abstractly as a shared normative system. Yet much of the commentary on subculture refers to behavior. In my judgment this identification is unwise. Behavior is the result of the convergence of many forces. One should not assume, when the members of a group behave in similar ways, that cultural norms produce this result. Collective behavior theory and personality theory may also help to account for the similarities.

CONTRACULTURE

Failure to distinguish between role and subculture and vagueness in the concept of culture itself are not the only difficulties in the use of the idea of subculture. Perhaps more serious is the tendency to obscure, under this one term, two levels of explanation, one sociological and the other social-psychological, with a resulting failure to understand the causal forces at work. On few topics can one get wider agreement among sociologists than on the dangers of reductionism. If a psychologist attempts to explain social facts by psychological theories, we throw the book (probably Durkheim) at him; we emphasize the "fallacy of misplaced concreteness." In view of the widespread neglect of socio-cultural factors in the explanation of behavior, this is a necessary task. It makes vitally important, however, keen awareness by sociologists that they also deal with an abstract model. Perhaps we can reverse Durkheim's dictum to say: Do not try to explain social psychological facts by sociological theories; or, more adequately, do not try to explain *behavior* (a product of the interaction of sociocultural and personality influences) by a sociological theory alone. Yablonsky has recently reminded us that an excessively sociological theory of gangs can result in our seeing a definite group structure and a clear pattern of norms where in fact there is a "near-group," with an imprecise definition of boundaries and limited agreement on norms.[6] Carelessly used, our concepts can obscure the facts we seek to understand.

To see the cultural element in delinquency or in the domination of an individual by his adolescent group, phenomena that on the surface are non-cultural or even "anti-cultural," was a long step forward in their explanation. But it is also necessary to see the non-cultural aspects of some "norms"—phenomena that on the surface seem thoroughly cultural. Our vocabulary needs to be rich enough to help us to deal with these differences. The tendency to use the same term to refer to phenomena that share *some* elements in common, disregarding important differences, is to be content with phyla names when we need also to designate genus and species.

To sharpen our analysis, I suggest the use of the term contra-culture wherever the normative system of a group contains, as a primary element, a theme of conflict with the values of the total society, where personality variables are directly involved in the development and maintenance of the group's values, and wherever its norms can be understood only by reference to the relationships of the group to a surrounding dominant culture.[7] None of these criteria definitely separates contraculture from subculture because each is a continuum. Sub-societies fall along a range with respect to each criterion. The values of most subcultures probably conflict in some measure with the larger culture. In a contraculture, however, the conflict element is central; many of the values, indeed, are specifically contradictions of the values of the dominant culture. Similarly, personality variables are involved in the development and maintenance of all cultures and subcultures, but usually the influence of personality is by way of variations around a theme that is part of the culture. In a contraculture, on the other hand, the theme itself expresses the tendencies of the persons who compose it. Finally, the norms of all subcultures are doubtless affected in some degree by the nature of the relationship with the larger culture. A subculture, as a pure type, however, does not require, for its understanding, intensive analysis of interaction with the larger culture; that is, its norms are not, to any significant degree, a product of that interaction. But a contraculture can be understood only by giving full attention to the interaction of the group which is its bearer with the larger society. . . .

Empirically, subcultural and contracultural influences may be mixed, of course. Delinquency and adolescent behavior almost certainly manifest both influences. The need, however, is to develop a clean analytic distinction between the two in order to interpret the wide variations in their mixture. . . .

DELINQUENT CONTRACULTURE

The usefulness of separating subcultural and contracultural influences is seen particularly clearly in the analysis of delinquency and of criminality generally. Perhaps in no other field were there more substantial gains in understanding made possible by the introduction of a sociological point of view to supplement and to correct individualistic and moralistic interpretations. There is little need to review the extensive literature, from *Delinquent Gangs* to *Delinquent Boys,* to establish the importance of the normative element in criminal and delinquent behavior. It is a mistake, however, to try to stretch a useful concept into a total theory. A "complex-adequate" analysis[8] may seem less sharp and definitive than one based on one factor, but it is likely to be far more useful. Cohen's excellent work,[9] although labelled as a study of the culture of the gang, does not overlook the psychogenic sources of delinquency. In fact, his explanation of the origins of the subculture (contraculture) and its functions for the lower class male makes clear that the norms of the gang are not learned, accepted, and taught in the same way that we learn what foods to eat, what clothes to wear, what language to speak. The very existence of the gang is a sign, in part, of blocked ambition. Because tensions set in motion by this blockage cannot be resolved by achievement of dominant values, such values are repressed, their importance denied, counter-values affirmed. The gang member is often ambivalent. Thwarted in his desire to achieve higher status by the criteria of the dominant society, he accepts criteria he can meet; but the reaction-formation in this response is indicated by the content of the delinquent norms—non-utilitarian, malicious, and nega-tivistic, in Cohen's terms. This negative polarity represents the need to repress his own tendencies to accept the dominant cultural standards. This is not to say that the values of the gang cannot be explained partially by cultural analysis, by some extension of the idea that "the mores can make anything right." But I suggest that Cohen's multiple-factor analysis might have been clearer, and less subject to misinterpretation, had he introduced the concept of contraculture alongside the concept of subculture. . . .

It should be stressed once more that these are analytic concepts, no one of which is adequate to handle the empirical variations of delinquent behavior. Failure to recognize the abstract quality of our conceptual tools leads to unnecessary disagreements. When Miller describes the "Lower Class Culture as a Generating Milieu of Gang Delinquency," for example, he points to an important series of influences that derive from the value system of the lower-class community.[10] In his effort to emphasize this aspect of the etiology of delinquency, however, he tends to overlook the kind of evidence reported by Sykes and Matza, Cohen, Finestone, Yablonsky, the McCords, and others concerning collective behavior and personality variables.[11] Surely the evidence is now rich enough for us to state definitively that delinquency is a multi-variable product. The task ahead is not to prove that it stems largely from cultural or subcultural or contracultural influences, but to spell out the conditions under which these and other factors will be found in various empirical mixtures.

CONTRACULTURAL ASPECTS OF CLASS AND OCCUPATION

The same admixture of the concepts of culture, subculture, and contraculture is found in the extensive literature on occupations and classes. Doubtless all three forces are found in many instances, and the research task is to untangle their various influences. It may stretch the meaning of the term too far to speak of the *position* of the "middle-class member," with its culturally designated role specifications; although in relatively stable societies the usage seems appropriate. In such societies, many of the rights and obligations of various status levels are culturally defined. In more mobile class systems, however, subcultural and contracultural norms become important. Our understanding of the American class system has certainly been deepened in the last twenty years by the descriptions of differences, among classes, in value perspectives, time orientations, levels of aspiration, leisure-time styles, and child rearing practices.

The introduction of the concept of subculture has helped to avoid class derived biasses in the interpretation of the wide variations in these phenomena. In class analysis as in the study of deviations, however, there may be some over-compensation in the effort to eliminate the distortions of a middle-class and often rural perspective.[12] There is evidence to suggest that differences between classes are based less upon different values and norms than the subcultural approach suggests. The "innovations" of lower-class members, to use Merton's term, are not simply subcultural acts defined as innovative by middle-class persons. They are in part responses to a frustrating situation. They are efforts to deal with the disjunction of means and ends. When the disjunction is reduced, the variations in value and behavior are reduced. Thus Rosen found, "surprisingly," that Negroes in the Northeast made higher scores on an "achievement value" test than his description of Negro "culture" led him to expect. This may indicate that the low achievement response is less the result of a subcultural norm than a protest against a difficult situation. If the situation improves, the achievement value changes.[13] Stephenson's discovery that occupational plans of lower-class youth are considerably below those of higher-class youth, but that their aspirations are only slightly lower, bears on this same point. His data suggest that the classes differ not only in norms, but also in opportunity.[14] Differences in behavior, therefore, are only partly a result of subcultural contrasts. The lower educational aspirations of lower-class members are also found to be in part situationally induced, not simply normatively induced. When the situation changes, values and behavior change, as Mulligan found in his study of the response of the sons of blue-collar workers to the educational opportunities of the GI Bill, and as Wilson reports in his investigation of the aspirations of lower-class boys attending higher-class schools and upper-class boys attending lower-class schools.[15]

In short, our thinking about differences in behavior among social classes will be sharpened if we distinguish among those differences that derive from role influences, those based on subcultural variations, and those that express contracultural responses to deprivation. The proportions will vary from society to society; the research task is to specify the conditions under which various distributions occur. One would expect, to propose one hypothesis, to find more contracultural norms among lower-class members of an open society than in a similar group in a closed society.

The interpretation of differential behavior among the members of various occupational categories can also be strengthened by the distinctions made above. Here the contrast between role and subculture is especially useful. The role of a teacher consists of the rights and duties that *integrate* him into a system of expected and established relationships with others. The teaching subculture, on the other hand, insofar as it exists, *separates* teachers from the cultural world of others. It is either unknown to others or, if known, a source of disagreement and perhaps of conflict with others. There are also contracultural aspects of some occupational styles of life. In interpreting the differences between the values of jazz musicians and "squares," for example, Becker writes: "their rejection of commercialism in music and squares in social life was part of the casting aside of the total American culture by men who could enjoy privileged status but who were unable to achieve a satisfactory personal adjustment within it."[16] Their style of life, in other words, can be understood only by supplementing the cultural and subcultural dimensions with the conflict theme. Cameron develops the same point. Although he makes no use of the term subculture, he describes the differentiating norms of the dance-band group, presumably a result of the "esoteric" aspects of their art, the differences in their time schedule, and the like. But he also describes the *contra* aspects of some of the norms, and suggests that they derive from the fact that early recruitment ties the jazz musician to the adolescence problem.[17]

CONCLUSION

Poorly defined terms plague research in many areas, particularly in the specification of relationships between sociological and social psychological levels of analysis. Thus "anomie" is still used to refer both to a social structural fact and to a personality fact, although this confusion is gradually being reduced. "Role" may refer, alternately, to rights and duties prescribed for the occupants of a position or to individual performance of that position. And subculture, I have suggested, is used to designate both the traditional norms of a sub-society and the emergent norms of a group caught in a frustrating and conflict-laden situation. This paper indicates that there are differences in the origin, function, and perpetuation of traditional and emergent norms, and suggests that the use of the concept contraculture for the latter might improve sociological analysis.

Hypotheses to guide the study of subculture can most profitably be derived from a general theory of culture. As an illustration, it may be hypothesized that a subculture will appear, in the first instance, as a result of mobility or an extension of communication that brings groups of different cultural background into membership in the same society, followed by physical or social isolation or both that prevents full assimilation.

Hypotheses concerning contracultures, on the other hand, can best be derived from social psychological theory—from the study of collective behavior, the frustration-aggression thesis, or the theory of group formation. One might hypothesize, for example, that under conditions of deprivation and frustration of major values (in a context where the deprivation is obvious because of extensive communication with the dominant group), and where value confusion and weak social controls obtain, contracultural norms will appear. One would expect to find, according to these propositions, many subcultural values among southern rural Negroes. Among first and second generation urban Negroes, however, one would expect an increase in contracultural norms. Both groups are deprived, but in the urban situation there is more "value leakage" from the dominant group, more value confusion, and weakened social controls.[18]

The subculture of the sociologist requires sophistication about the full range of human behavior. This desideratum has led to the propositon that the vast diversity of norms believed in and acted upon by the members of a modern society is not a sign of value confusion and breakdown but rather an indication that urban life brings into one system of interaction persons drawn from many cultural worlds. One unanticipated consequence of the sociological subculture may be that we exaggerate the normative insulation and solidarity of these various worlds. An important empirical question concerns the extent and results of their interaction.

FOOTNOTES

[1]There are a few formal definitions. For example: "The term 'subculture' refers in this paper to 'cultural variants displayed by certain segments of the population.' Subcultures are distinguished not by one or two isolated traits—they constitute relatively cohesive cultural systems. They are worlds within the larger world of our national culture." (Mirra Komarovsky and S. S. Sargent, "Research into Subcultural Influences upon Personality," in S. S. Sargent and M. W. Smith, editors, *Culture and Personality,* New York: The Viking Fund, 1949, 143.) These authors then refer to class, race, occupation, residence, and region. After referring to sub-group values and language, Kimball Young and Raymond W. Mack state: "Such shared learned behaviors which are common to

a specific group or category are called *subcultures."* *(Sociology and Social Life,* New York: American Book, 1959, 49.) They refer then to ethnic, occupational, and regional variations. Blaine Mercer writes: "A society contains numerous subgroups, each with its own characteristic ways of thinking and acting. These cultures within a culture are called *subcultures." (The Study of Society,* New York: Harcourt-Brace, 1958, 34.) Thereafter he discusses Whyte's *Streetcorner Society.* Although these definitions are helpful, they fail to make several distinctions which are developed below.

[2]A. L. Kroeber, "The Concept of Culture in Science," *Journal of General Education* (April, 1949), 187....

[3]Ralph Linton, *The Study of Man,* New York: Appleton-Century, 1936, 486...

[4]Edward Sapir, "Personality," in *Encyclopedia of the Social Sciences,* New York: Macmillan, 1931, Vol. 12, 86; Charles H. Cooley, *Human Nature and the Social Order,* revised edition, New York: Scribner, 1922.

[5]It is possible, of course, for a subculture to specify roles within its own system.

[6]Lewis Yablonsky, "The Delinquent Gang as a Near-Group," *Social Problems* (Fall, 1959), 108–117.

[7]By the noun in "contraculture" I seek to call attention to the normative aspects of the phenomena under study and by the qualifying prefix to call attention to the conflict aspects....

[8]See Robin M. Williams, Jr., "Continuity and Change in Sociological Study," *American Sociological Review* (December, 1958), 619–633.

[9]Albert K. Cohen, *Delinquent Boys,* Glencoe, Ill.: Free Press, 1955.

[10]Walter B. Miller, "Lower Class Culture as a Generating Milieu of Gang Delinquency," *The Journal of Social Issues* (1958), 5–19.

[11]In addition to the studies of Cohen and Yablonsky cited above, see Gresham M. Sykes and David Matza, "Techniques of Neutralization: A Theory of Delinquency," *American Sociological Review* (December, 1957), 664-670; Harold Finestone, "Cats, Kicks, and Color", *Social Problems* (July, 1957), 3-13; and William McCord and Joan McCord, *Origins of Crime. A New Evaluation of the Cambridge-Somerville Youth Study,* New York: Columbia University, 1959.

[12]C. Wright Mills, "The Professional Ideology of Social Pathologists," *American Journal of Sociology* (September, 1943), 165–180.

[13]Bernard C. Rosen, "Race, Ethnicity, and the Achievement Syndrome," *American Sociological Review* (February, 1959), 47–60....

[14]Richard M. Stephenson, "Mobility Orientation and Stratification of 1,000 Ninth Graders," *American Sociological Review* (April, 1957), 204–212.

[15]Raymond A. Mulligan, "Socio-Economic Background and College Enrollment," *American Sociological Review* (April, 1951), 188–196; Alan B. Wilson, "Residential Segregation of Social Classes and Aspirations of High School Boys," *American Sociological Review* (December, 1959), 836–845.

[16]Howard S. Becker, "The Professional Dance Musician and His Audience," *American Journal of Sociology* (September, 1951), 136–144.

[17]W. B. Cameron, "Sociological Notes on the Jam Session," *Social Forces* (December, 1954), 177–182.

[18]There are numerous alternative ways in which the protest against deprivation can be expressed. Delinquency and drug addiction often have a

contracultural aspect; but somewhat less clearly, political and religious movements among disprivileged groups may also invert the values of the influential but inaccessible dominant group. Thus the concept of contraculture may help us to understand, for example, the Garveyite movement, the Ras Tafari cult, and some aspects of the value schemes of lower-class sects. (See, e.g., Liston Pope, *Millhands and Preachers,* New Haven: Yale University Press, 1942; and George E. Simpson, "The Ras Tafari Movement in Jamaica: A study of Race and Class Conflict," *Social Forces* (December, 1955), 167–170.)

12

SUBCULTURE OF VIOLENCE: AN INTEGRATED CONCEPTUALIZATION

Marvin E. Wolfgang and Franco Ferracuti

Although, or perhaps because, the term 'subculture' has been used by anthropologists and sociologists in a variety of ways and contexts, it contains much ambiguity. There is a reasonable degree of consensus in its use among sociologists, but other social scientists and psychologists may be less familiar with its implications. The prefix 'sub' refers only to a subcategory of culture, a part of the whole; it does not necessarily indicate a derogation unless a particular subculture is viewed as undesirable by the members of the dominant or a contrary value system. For analytical purposes, the sociologist uses the term without a value judgement. In this section we seek to analyze the meaning of 'subculture' and to discuss its definition, with the hope that its conceptual meaning may be made more clear for future theory and research. . . .

Reprinted with permission of authors and publisher from *The Subculture of Violence*, Tavistock Publications, Inc. (London), 1967, pp. 95-113; 164-167; 314-315.

THE SUBCULTURE IN RELATION
TO THE DOMINANT CULTURE

A subculture implies that there are value judgements or a social value system which is apart from and a part of a larger or central value system. From the viewpoint of this larger dominant culture, the values of the subculture set the latter apart and prevent total integration, occasionally causing open or covert conflicts. The dominant culture may directly or indirectly promote this apartness, of course, and the degree of reciprocal integration may vary, but whatever the reason for the difference, normative isolation and solidarity of the subculture result. There are shared values that are learned, adopted, and even exhibited by participants in the subculture, and that differ in quantity and quality from those of the dominant culture. Just as man is born into a culture, so he may be born into a subculture.

A subculture is only partly different from the parent culture. We use the term 'parent' to refer both to a larger culture from which subcultural elements have stemmed as different offshoots of its own value system and to a larger culture that is willing to adopt a subculture voluntarily grafted to the parent because of a sufficiency in number and type of significant values commonly shared between 'parent' and 'child.' Occasionally this 'adoption' is the almost chance result of political events or of geographical proximity, but still a certain degree, however minimal, of acceptance is necessary. In one sense, the labor union movement that grew up within America was spawned by values inherent but long dormant in the dominant culture and is an example of the first type. The Hasidic Jews in Williamsburg[1] represent a parental cultural adoption. In either case, the subculture by any definition or classification cannot be *totally* different from the culture of which it is a part. The problem of what really defines 'difference' in a culture in today's world of relatively free interchange of opinions and values remains to be solved. Even very different societies from a political and ethnic viewpoint tend to have some common values and behavioral patterns.

Some of the values of a subculture may, however, more than differ from those of the larger culture. They may also be in conflict or at variance with the latter. It may be useful for our analysis to distinguish, as Yinger has done, between subcultures and contracultures. He refers to subcultures as systems which embody values only different from but not antithetical to the broader social system; and to contracultures as those subcultures which have values at variance with the dominant value system. We must again emphasize that no subculture can be totally different from or completely in conflict with the society of which it is a part. The 'conflict' stems from a contrast of two or more normative systems, at least one of which implies strong adherence to a set of moral values that are often codified. To be part of the larger culture implies that some values related to the ends or means of the whole are shared by the part. The subculture that is only different is a tolerated deviation. Values which a culture can tolerate are those that do not cause disruptive conflict or that do not disturb too much the larger normative solidarity. Moreover, tolerated values are not functionally necessary for maintaining allegiance to the core values of the culture. Even a subculture can tolerate values outside its value system so long as they do not disturb allegiance to its own basic values that distinguish it as a subculture, and as long as its own existence, or the existence of its leaders and opinion-makers, is not menaced.

CONDUCT NORMS

The values shared in a subculture are often made evident and can be identified phenomenologically in terms of the conduct that is expected, ranging from the permissible to the required, in certain kinds of life situation. Again, Sellin has noted: 'Some of these life situations, at least, are sufficiently repetitious and socially so defined that they call for definite responses from the type of person who encounters them. There are attached to them, so to speak, norms which define the reaction or response which in a given person is approved or disapproved by the normative group. The social attitude of this group toward the various ways in which a person might act under certain circumstances has thus been crystallized into a rule, the violation of which arouses a group reaction. These rules or norms may be called *conduct norms.* [2] Conduct of an individual is, then, an external exhibition of sharing in (sub) cultural values, and this form of manifestation of values would surely satisfy Durkheim's emphasis on 'facts' that have the quality of exteriority. The norms that govern conduct will involve varying degrees of expectation of individual conformity to the shared values. The same norms may serve as criteria for defining what is 'normal' or expected conduct and what is not. Abnormal may then be further classified into 'bad' or 'immoral' and 'sick' or 'maladjusted' or psychologically ill, or combinations thereof.

When we speak of the 'teenage culture,' the 'adolescent culture,' or even the 'delinquent subculture,' we have not yet stated whether we are discussing quantitative variables or qualitative attributes or both. We have not isolated sufficiently the differentiating normative items. The persuasive and provocative arguments about a delinquent subculture that emerge from a working-class ethic are only beginnings toward establishing operational hypotheses, which are needed but which cannot be tested until we have objective and independent measurements of the norms of conduct. Until further clarification is made, Kluckhohn's reference to 'the subculture of anthropologists,' Riesman's use of a 'subculture among the faculty,' or reference to any other type of 'subculture' cannot easily be rejected as too loose usages of the term.

SOCIAL GROUPS

It is difficult to discuss subcultures and conduct norms without reference to social groups. Values are shared by individuals and individuals sharing values make up groups. In most cases when we refer to subcultures (the Amish, Hutterites, the earlier ghettoes, delinquent conflict gangs) we are thinking of individuals sharing common values and socially interacting in some limited geographical or residential isolation. However, value-sharing does not necessarily require social interaction. Consequently a subculture may exist, widely distributed spatially and without interpersonal contact among individuals or whole groups of individuals. Several delinquent gangs may be spread throughout a city and rarely or never have contacts. Yet they are referred to collectively as the 'delinquent subculture,' and properly so, for otherwise each gang would have to be considered a separate subculture. Individual (non-group) behavior can be subcultural so long as it reflects values of an existing subculture.

Members of a group use one another as reference points for self-image and for establishing the relationship of self to others. This process implies continuing reinforcement of the subcultural values. A wish to remain an ingroup participant does not necessarily mean, however, a total personal commitment or commitment to the totality of subcultural values. The individual may occasionally be more concerned with maintaining his group association than with sharing the group's values. He may be reluctant to exhibit his group allegiance in a way that is discordant with his own beliefs, but at the same time he may place a higher value on remaining a member of the group than on abrogating the prescriptions of conduct. The juvenile who conforms to the delinquent gang's demands for fighting but who dislikes the resort to violence, and the soldier who goes to combat with deep hatred for war are both unwilling to sever association with their groups but cannot be said to share much in the value of violence. The value these two individuals will share with their groups is that of maintaining the group. Thus, while the manifest representation (conduct) of the subculture may generally be a valid index of normatively induced values, latent and different values may be retained by some individuals who are members of the group that share in this subculture. Several degrees of conflicting situation may occur, and the resulting psychodynamics may find expression in personal psychological disturbances ranging from simple anxiety to more malignant reactions. The need for assessment of the deep personal affiliations and motives decreases reliance on external behavior, or 'facts,' for determining cultural and subcultural allegiances in specific individuals.

Because a subculture refers to a normative system of some group or groups smaller than the whole society, it should be possible to examine descriptively the composition of the population that shares the subcultural values. Individuals are, after all, culture-carriers who both reflect and transmit through social learning, the attitudes, ideals, and ideas of their cultures. A subcultural ethos may be shared by all ages. Still, that ethos may be most prominent in a limited, segmental age group. Furthermore, if beyond typical role differentiations there are also normatively induced sex role expectations and social class variations, we may further refine and localize the strongest and most visible group reflecting the subcultural value or values. Although conduct, as we have noted, may not invariably be in accord with the actor's attitude, the social analyst often has little more than forms of conduct to examine and uses them as representations of group values. If a form of conduct is most commonly found among a limited portion of the population, if the conduct is deviant from the dominant culture prescriptions and possesses the other aspects we have considered thus far in our analysis of subcultures, then we should expect to learn something tangible, objective, and empirical about the parameters of the subculture, its etiology, its strength and likelihood of persistence, and how it might be cultivated, modified, or eliminated. To limit ourselves to the external parameters of 'conduct' does not necessarily exclude further 'depth' analysis, but offers a consistent starting-point which can be used to delimit our research 'population.'

ROLES

An analytical distinction between role norms and subculture has been suggested by Yinger.[3] But because many role norms are defined within a subcultural complex, the distinction is often empirically unclear. The rights and duties assigned to a specific role in the larger culture may simply be exaggerated, extended, or distorted in the subcultural normative system so that the differences, instead of being sharp, are variable and sometimes situational. For example, the male role may be legally and functionally similar both in the dominant culture and in a particular subculture, but the latter may assign rights to the role that were formerly, but are no longer, aspects of the male role in the dominant culture. Or the different language, drinking habits, sex behavior, leisure pursuits, etc., of males who share subcultural values may be role expectations normatively induced.

Role differentiation exists in all societies, but only heterogeneous societies can have subcultures.[4] And because social interaction in an open society can involve an individual's participation in a considerable diversity of groups, there may be a number of subcultures to which he has commitments so long as these subcultures do not conflict or so long as the individual can withstand the stress of the resulting conflict. The various subcultures in which an individual is involved generally must be complementary or supplementary; otherwise his personality might become unintegrated or disintegrated. Occasionally, life situations will cause psychological disintegration through enforced participation in conflicting sets of values, as can often be the case in migrating groups. If these assumptions are correct, we can assume the presence of common subcultural themes, or normative aspects, that appear in some or all of the subcultures in which the individual shares values. With the same thread he weaves his way through and ties together more than one set of values. He can do this because each set has some common link with every other set. Specific value elements will not appear in all sets because of their limitation to only one set. But we have already said that a subculture must have some major values in common with the dominant culture in order to be designated a *sub*culture, otherwise the prefix indicating connective values should be dropped. Therefore, some minimal similarity must also exist between (or among) subcultures in which an individual is immersed.

SITUATIONAL AND SUBCULTURAL NORMS

Some ideas, attitudes, means, goals, or conduct may be 'situationally induced, not simply normatively induced.'[5] If the situation changes, in these circumstances, presumably values and behavior change, thus indicating no real and enduring normative allegiance. This is not an entirely satisfactory distinction. If it were, the issue would then be how permanent the situation has been or might be, or, particularly, whether attitude or behavior is unisituational, i.e. whether there is only a single situation that induces a typically common response. The statistical rather than the subcultural norm is more likely to be used in analysis of behavioral reactions to a specific situation. For a response to be normatively induced, it seems that we must resort to such a phrase as 'style of life' in order to indicate the pervasiveness involved in the normative character of action. But again, what this means quantitatively and empirically is that the action at least must be multisituational. If we were to use permanence of a social response as a criterion of normativeness, any modification of the norm would require our classifying it ex post facto as situational. But if values change when situations change, it is also likely that situations change when values change, or that varied adherence to the values causes a differential choice of situations on the part of the individual.

We are suggesting, then, that a given conduct norm or a set of values must function to govern the conduct in a variety of situations in order to classify that norm or value-set as a (sub)culturally expected or required response and not merely as a statistical modal reaction. This suggestion means that we must examine many different kinds of personal and social interaction to establish a firm empirical basis for the classification. The resulting categories will be meaningful from a psychological standpoint as well as from a pure sociological perspective. Moreover, the presence, even in a latent sense, of potential employment of a normatively induced and supported response calls attention to the pervasive, penetrating, and diffusive character of the response. An individual carrier of a norm may be consciously or subconsciously prepared to react in the same way in various social situations, or does in fact react similarly in diverse circumstances. The reaction may differ phenotypically, but the choice of the 'problem-relieving' mechanism may be the same. The degree of the individual's assimilation of the norm may in part be measured by the number and kinds of situations in which he uses the norm as supportive explanation for his behavior. . . .

TRANSMISSION OF VALUES

The transmission of subcultural values obviously involves analysis of the personality factors of individual participants. The 'sharing of values' means that there has been a learning process that established a dynamic lasting linkage between the values and the individuals. It is at this point of analysis that the psychological theory of personality and the sociological theories of subcultures can best be integrated both with one another and with empirical data. Whether or not a subculture is principally the product of interaction with the dominant culture, whether or not the primary element of a subculture is a contradiction of, or is in conflict with, the larger culture, personality variables are involved in the acceptance or rejection of the whole or a part of the subcultural values. Allowing for individual variations, the learning process must have generated common 'motives,' common reaction patterns, and differential perceptual habits. Occasional evidence of the differential psychology of members of a subculture is available, but it has seldom been linked to a general subcultural frame of reference.

THE PROBLEM OF QUANTIFICATION

. . . What criteria can be used to provide findings that would enable us to designate a set of values as subcultural, particularly in the field of criminology? First, if a subculture is denoted by values that are different from those of the dominant culture, we should determine whether the values are (a) tolerated differences that are not disruptive, that do not cause injury or possess potential threat of social injury to the dominant culture; or are (b) conflicting differences that are disruptive, that do cause injury or possess potential threat of social injury to the dominant culture. The Amish in Pennsylvania share values that by and large are tolerated deviations from American culture; however, there are a few values that the Amish possess that are much at variance and in conflict with the larger culture.[6] The 'delinquent subculture' is characterized principally by conduct that reflects values antithetical to the surrounding culture; but a variety of their activities are acceptable juvenile and not delinquent behavior. The different but tolerated values are concordant with the broader culture themes, for the two flow together without discord and the one is but an exaggeration of or an addendum to the other. The conflicting values are discordant and negative because of their disrupting effect upon the broader culture themes.[7] We are, therefore, suggesting at this point that there are two major types of subcultural values: (a) *tolerated concordant values;* and (b) *untolerated discordant values.*

This suggested dichotomy is commonly recognized, but has not been made explicit or described value by value in sufficient detail. It calls, first, for a classification of norms assumed to be different in *kind.* But before this division can be empirically performed, we need clear ideas of the values that constitute the dominant value system so that we have a base line from which to determine the category of values that presumably are different. The process of classifying values becomes the first and necessary task leading toward measurement of value differentiation. As has been suggested, 'Any classification . . . serves no more purpose than the catalog of events in chemistry, but without such a catalog, the study of combination of norms, their relationship to other cultural phenomena, etc., cannot be placed on a high scientific plane and thus aid in the scientific description of the phenomena of social life.'

Second, the *number* of values that a subculture possesses that are different from those of the dominant culture is important, but only as each is considered in relation to its similar or antithetical value in the dominant culture. Thus a prerequisite of establishing the parameters of a subculture would appear to be the construction of a scale of values in the dominant culture. This scaling seems necessary if we are to weigh the importance of particular variant values or of their interacting patterns. For instance, two values that conflict with the larger culture may be of supreme evaluative importance to the latter; the apposition, therefore, could be sufficient to constitute a subculture. On the other hand, ten untolerated and discordant values may be of little importance and should consequently be viewed relative to the position of the previous two. This may be an individual, temporary phenomenon which calls for analysis of another area; i.e. the *stability* of a subculture. Relating a subcultural value element by the position of its directly opposite value in the hierarchy of the scale of values of the dominant culture might be part of the measurement process. If the subcultural element is a tolerated concordant value, relating it to the distance from the position of the parent value from which it is an offshoot would be one aid in measurement.

We should be able to measure the degree of value variance in terms of the reactions of agents of the dominant culture, according to whether they view a subcultural difference with tolerance or see variance as an actual or potential threat to the value of the dominant culture. An attitude scale could be used to obtain data on the direction (tolerated concordant vs. untolerated discordant) and on the extent to which subcultural values or conduct norms are thought to differ from the larger culture values. The perspective of a group representative of the dominant value system could help to determine the degree of variance. (Temporal, situational variations in the group perspectives would have to be taken into account.)

The *intensity or strength* of a value is conceived as a measurable item. We are here referring to the extent to which the value is internalized, absorbed, and consequently shared by agents of the subculture. An attitude scale could be constructed to register the degree of allegiance owed by members of a subculture to subcultural values. This could be done with the help of attitude-measuring through questionnaires, as has been attempted by Reckless, or, at a deeper level of personality assessment, through analysis of values and social motives derived from projective instruments.

Sellin has suggested that the intrinsic quality of a norm might be measurable in degrees. We have noted that he refers to this inherent energy or power of the norm as its resistance potential. He adds: 'This quality could perhaps be utilized as one basis for a preliminary and experimental classification of norms. Its utility would, of course, depend on the development of some technique of measurement, whereby conduct norms, regardless of the group evolving them, could be fitted into divisions on a scale.'[9] We have earlier referred to deviations within each subculture. The sanctions applied to these deviations can provide some measurement of the strength of the conduct norm based entirely upon the degree of severity of the penalty assigned to the violations. Deviations within a subcultural value system that have the same penalty would be grouped together and would carry the same weight, regardless of any other characteristics of these offenses.

It could be argued that we might establish a scale of values for the dominant culture in much the same way; i.e. by measuring the severity of the penalty ('resistance potential') for deviations from conduct norms. Although this position might be valid for legal norms generally, sanctions assigned for deviations from non-legal norms reflecting non-legal values would probably be extremely difficult to designate, and might have entirely different strengths and connotations in similar but geographically separated subcultures. A dominant culture that can exist with a variety of satellite subcultures will itself be heterogeneous and characterized by mobile degrees of support or mild rebuke within the range of acceptable conduct. Conformity generally is less required and demanded by the dominant culture than by any subculture, and the number, range, and variety of alternative forms of conduct are probably greater in the larger culture. Likewise, in the larger culture there is range and variety to the informal modes of control (sanctions) assigned to deviations that do not themselves amount to subcultural variations. To maintain its distinctive form of value differentiation, to preserve its identity, a subculture must generally attach stronger demands for conformity to those very value elements that are different from those of the larger culture. Because these different values are but a part of a subcultural system that mostly shares the values of the dominant culture (else, as we have said, it could not be a part of the whole), they are relatively few and the sanctions assigned to deviations from them should be more obvious and measurable. Thus we are suggesting that either a scaling analysis of individual attitudes of allegiance to subcultural values, or a scaling analysis of penalties for deviations from subcultural norms, could be used to provide a measure of the intensity or strength of subcultural values. . . .

SUMMARY

In brief, the theory of a subculture of violence does not include all aggression, socialized or not; it does not include all crime or even all criminal homicide. It does include most aggression manifested in physical assaults that are prohibited in criminal codes under such designations as homicide and assaults.

The notions of a subculture of violence are built upon existing (a) sociological theory on culture, social and personality systems, culture conflict, differential association, and value systems; (b) psychological theory on learning, conditioning, developmental socialization, differential identification; and (c) criminological research on criminal homicide and other assaultive crimes.

The principal propositions of the theory, we have said in Chapter III, include the following, some of which apply in part to the meaning of all subcultures:

1. No subculture can be totally different from or totally in conflict with the society of which it is a part.

2. To establish the existence of a subculture of violence does not require that the actors sharing in this basic value element express violence in all situations.

3. The potential resort or willingness to resort to violence in a variety of situations emphasizes the penetrating and diffusive nature of this culture theme.

4. The subcultural ethos of violence may be shared by all ages in a subsociety, but this ethos is most prominent in a limited age group ranging from late adolescence to middle age.

5. The counter-norm is nonviolence.

6. The development of favorable attitudes toward, and the use of, violence in this subculture involve learned behavior and a process of differential learning, association, or identification.

7. The use of violence in a subculture is not necessarily viewed as illicit conduct, and the users therefore do not have to deal with feelings of guilt about their aggression.

Hypotheses included in these propositions and that constitute suggestions for further research are the following:

1. The parameters of a subculture of violence can be partly established by measurement of social values using a ratio scale (as in psychophysics) focused on items concerned with the

behavioral displays of violence.

2. Psychometric and projective techniques show high correlations between their assessment of aggression and the psychophysical scale scores.

3. Social correlates of criminal assaultive behavior have high correlations with the psychometric and projective techniques and with the psychophysical scale scores.

4. By means of these scale scores and techniques, it is possible to designate the personality and social attributes of the representatives of a subculture of violence, which in turn makes possible the identification of ecological areas and boundaries of the subculture that interact with the dominant culture.

5. Such designated actors and identified regions allow for significantly accurate predictions to be made about future violent criminal behavior among (a) persons who have not yet engaged in such behavior, or (b) persons who have previously committed at least one assaultive crime that has come to the attention of the public authorities.

6. Persons not members of a subculture of violence who none the less commit crimes of violence have psychological and social attributes significantly different from violent criminals from the subculture of violence; i.e. violent criminal offenders from a culture of nonviolence have more psychopathological traits, more guilt, and more anxiety about their violent behavior.

7. Predictable and positive prevention of additional crimes of violence is possible by social action that is designed (a) to disperse, disrupt, and disorganize the representatives of the subculture of violence, and at the same time (b) to effect changes in the value system.

8. Therapy in correctional institutions is most effective with assaultive offenders from a subculture of violence if (a) the offenders are not permitted to retain their collective and supportive homogeneity in prison; (b) values contrary to the subculture of violence are infused into their personality structure and into the prison social system with clarity and commitment by the therapists; (c) these inmates are brought to the

point of anomic anxiety; and (*d*) they are not returned to their subculture of origin.

FOOTNOTES

[1]Solomon Poll, *The Hasidic Community of Williamsburg,* New York: The Free Press of Glencoe, 1962.

[2]Thorsten Sellin, *Culture Conflict and Crime,* New York: Social Science Research Council, Bulletin 41, 1938, 28.

[3]Milton Yinger, "Contraculture and Subculture," *American Sociological Review* (October, 1960), 625–635.

[4]*Ibid.,* 627.

[5]*Ibid.,* 634.

[6]See for example, John A. Hostetler, *Amish Society,* Baltimore: Johns Hopkins Press, 1963.

[7]The analyst is not necessarily required to determine whether description may have ultimately good or bad effects if these effects should change the larger culture. Such a determination would obviously involve an ethical judgement.

[8]Sellin, *op. cit.,* 35.

[9]*Ibid.,* 34.

13

THE SUBSOCIETY AND
THE SUBCULTURE

Milton M. Gordon

By the social structure of a society I mean the set of crystallized
social relationships which its members have with each other which
places them in groups, large or small, permanent or temporary,
formally organized or unorganized, and which relates them to the
major institutional activities of the society, such as economic and
occupational life, religion, marriage and the family, education, government, and recreation. To study a society's social structure is to study
the nature of its family groups, its age and sex distribution and the
social groupings based on these categories, its social cliques, its formal
and informal organizations, its divisions on the basis of race, religion,
and national origin, its social classes, its urban and rural groups, and
the pattern of social relationships in school and college, on the job,

Reprinted with permission of author and publisher from *Assimilation in
American Life*, Oxford University Press, 1964, pp. 30-54.

in the church, in voting behavior and political participation, and in leisure time activities. It is a large definition but a consistent one in that it focuses on *social relationships,* and social relationships that are *crystallized*—that is, which are not simply occasional and capricious but have a pattern of some repetition and can to some degree be predicted, and are based, at least to some extent, on a set of shared expectations. . . .

Social structure, man's crystallized social relationships, is one side of the coin of human life, the other side of which is *culture.* Culture, as the social scientist uses the term, refers to the social heritage of man—the ways of acting and the ways of doing things which are passed down from one generation to the next, not through genetic inheritance but by formal and informal methods of teaching and demonstration. The classic definition of culture is that of the early anthropologist, E. B. Tylor, who described it as "that complex whole which includes knowledge, belief, art, morals, law, custom, and any other capabilities and habits acquired by man as a member of society.[1] Culture, in other words, is the way of life of a society, and if analyzed further is seen to consist of prescribed ways of behaving or norms of conduct, beliefs, values, and skills, along with the behavioral patterns and uniformities based on these categories—all this we call "non-material culture"—plus, in an extension of the term, the artifacts created by these skills and values, which we call "material culture."

Culture and social structure are obviously closely related and in a constant state of dynamic interaction, for it is the norms and values of the society which, for the most part, determine the nature of the social groupings and social relationships which its members will create; and, conversely, frequently it is through the action of men in social groups that cultures undergo change and modification. To illustrate the first point we need only think of the adult organizations so characteristic of American life (and which we take for granted) composed of adults of both sexes, married and unmarried, who come together because of some common interest. An example would be a municipal choral society, a poetry club, or a chapter of the American Civil Liberties Union. An organization composed in this fashion would be unthinkable in a traditional Moslem society. To illustrate the second point, we may note that it was an organization, The Bolshevik Party under Lenin, which provided the dynamic thrust that produced the vast cultural changes that constitute the enormous behavioral gap between Czarist Russia during World War I and the Soviet Union of the 1960's.

When used in the general sense, the term "culture" refers to the sum of man's social heritage existing over the world at any given time. More frequently, however, the term is used specifically to refer to the social heritage or way of life of a particular human society at a particular time. Thus one speaks of American culture in the twentieth century, as differentiated, for instance, from French culture in the eighteenth century, or from contemporary Chinese culture. It is obvious, then, that the term may be applied to human groupings of various dimensions, whenever these groupings involve shared behavioral norms and patterns that differ somewhat from those of other groups. Thus in one sense, America, France, and Italy are all a part of Western culture because of certain behavioral values shared by Americans, Frenchmen, and Italians as the result of their common social heritage of European life—values which they do not share with peoples of Oriental or African cultural background. By the same token, groups *within* a national society may differ somewhat in their cultural values since in a large, modern, complex, multigroup nation, cultural uniformity of the type approximated in a primitive society is impossible of attainment. Thus we may speak of the culture of a group smaller than the national society.

THE SUBSOCIETY AND THE SUBCULTURE

With these concepts of "social structure" and "culture" in mind, we may now go on to develop the argument. The ethnic group, I have said, bears a special relationship to the social structure of a modern complex society which distinguishes it from all small groups and most other large groups. It is this: *within the ethnic group there develops a network of organizations and informal social relationships which permits and encourages the members of the ethnic group to remain within the confines of the group for all of their primary relationships and some of their secondary relationships throughout all the stages of the life-cycle.* From the cradle in the sectarian hospital to the child's play group, to the social clique in high school, the fraternity and religious center in college, the dating group within which he searches for a spouse, the marriage partner, the neighborhood of residence, the church affiliation and the church clubs, the men's and the women's social and service clubs, the adult clique of "marrieds," the vacation resort, and then as the age-cycle nears completion, the rest home for the elderly and, finally, the sectarian cemetery—in all of these activities and relationships which are close to the core of personality and selfhood—the member of the ethnic group may, if he wishes, and will in fact in many cases, follow a path which never takes him across the boundaries of his ethnic subsocietal network.

In addition, some of the basic institutional activities of the larger society become either completely or in part ethnically enclosed. Family life and religion are, virtually by definition, contained within the ethnic boundaries. Education becomes ethnically enclosed to the extent that "parochial" school systems are utilized. Even within public and nonsectarian private schools and colleges, a system of social cliques and voluntary religious organizations set up for educational and social purposes may effectively separate the students from each other in all but formal classroom instruction. Economic and occupational activities, based as they are on impersonal market relationships, defy ethnic enclosure in the United States more than any institution except the political or governmental, but even here a considerable degree of ethnic enclosure is by no means a rarity. The white Christian who works for an all-white Christian business concern, or the Jew who is employed by an all-Jewish firm, labors at the points of intersection of the economic institution and ethnicity. Even in the "all-ethnic" business concern, impersonal secondary relationships across ethnic group lines may take place in wholesale purchasing or in sales. However, if the clientele of the concern is also of the same ethnic group—examples would be the kosher butchershop or the retail store whose only merchandise is religious objects for Catholic consumption—then the isolation from inter-ethnic contacts even on the job is virtually complete.

Governmental relationships to the larger society are, by definition, non-ethnically oriented. That is, barring the exceptions noted earlier, the politico-legal system of the United States recognizes no distinctions on the basis of race, religion, or national origin, and a citizen's obligations, responsibilities, and relationships to the laws of the state are not ethnically qualified.[2] Active work in political parties, if it is above the local neighborhood level (and frequently even there), takes one across ethnic group lines. "Bloc voting" on an ethnic basis has, of course, played an important part in American political affairs, and although the day of herding masses of unknowing immigrants to the polls is past, ethnic background still influences voting preferences in substantial fashion,[3] even though it is a reasonable guess that, over the long run, time and increasing socioeconomic differentiation within each ethnic group will gradually dilute the ethnic impact on politics. Military service, since the banishment of racial segregation from the armed forces, mixes people of varying ethnic backgrounds indiscriminately.

I shall return to this subject in greater detail later and discuss exceptions, individual and patterned, to the "model" of American society which I am presenting, but here my purpose is to paint the picture in broad strokes. In these terms, as far as we have gone, the American social structure may be seen, then, as a national society which contains within its political boundaries a series of *subsocieties* based on ethnic identity. The network of organizations, informal social relationships, and institutional activities which makes up the ethnic subsociety tends to pre-empt most or all primary group relationships, while secondary relationships across ethnic group lines are carried out in the "larger society," principally in the spheres of economic and occupational life, civic and political activity, public and private nonparochial education, and mass entertainment. All of these relationships, primary and secondary, are contained within the boundaries of common political allegiance and responsibility to the politico-legal demands and expectations of American nationality. . . .

Thus far we have called attention to two functional characteristics of the ethnic group or subsociety. First, it serves psychologically as a source of group self-identification—the locus of the sense of intimate peoplehood—and second, it provides a patterned network of groups and institutions which allows an individual to confine his primary group relationships to his own ethnic group throughout all the stages of the life cycle. Its third functional characteristic is that it refracts the national cultural patterns of behavior and values through the prism of its own cultural heritage. This unique sub-national heritage may consist of cultural norms brought over from the country of recent emigration, it may rest on different religious values, or on the cumulative domestic experiences of enforced segregation as a group within American borders over a number of generations, or on some combination of these sources of cultural diversity. It is this phenomenon which is patently the basis for the term "cultural pluralism," used to describe the model of American society as a composite of groups which have preserved their own cultural identity. The question of the actual extent of this cultural diversity in contemporary American society I wish to leave for later discussion. My purpose here is simply to point out that provision for the possibility of cultural diversity within the larger national society is the third major functional characteristic of the ethnic subsociety. In this sense, then, just as we speak of the national culture as representing the cultural way of life or cultural patterns of the national society, one may think of the ethnic subsociety as having its own cultural patterns, these patterns consisting of the national cultural patterns blended with or refracted through the particular cultural heritage of the ethnic group; this blend or amalgam we may call, in preliminary fashion, the *subculture* of the ethnic subsociety.

The term "subculture" has been used by a number of sociologists to refer to the cultural patterns of any subgroup or type of subgroup within the national society. One may speak of the subculture of a gang, a neighborhood, a factory, a hospital, etc. Albert K. Cohen's excellent study of delinquency in which he analyzes the cultural patterns of the delinquent gang is based on such a use of the term.[4] We prefer, however, to reserve the term "subculture" to stand for the cultural patterns of a subsociety which contains both sexes, all ages, and family groups, and which parallels the larger society in that it provides for a network of groups and institutions extending throughout the individual's entire life cycle. For the cultural patterns of a group more restricted in scope than an entire subsociety we suggest the term "groupculture."[5] The distinction allows us to isolate and distinguish from each other phenomena of different scope and import. It is summarized briefly in the paradigm presented in Table [1].

Table 1. Social Units and their Cultures

Social Unit	Cultural Term
The National Society (or The Society): (The nation with its political boundaries)	The National Culture (or The Culture)
The Subsociety (the social unit, smaller than the national society, which contains a large network of groups and institutions extending through the entire life cycle of the individual)	The Subculture
The Group (groups of segmental import; for example, the gang, the play-group, the factory, the hospital, the office.	The Groupculture

Thus far I have spoken of the subsociety as though it were equivalent to the ethnic group. However, if we stop to consider the functional characteristics of the subsociety—its salience as a locus of group identification, its network of groups and institutions which allow primary group relationships to be confined within its borders throughout the life cycle, and its role as a carrier of particular cultural patterns, then it becomes clear that other sociological categories, in addition to the ethnic group, demand consideration. The rise of the city created differences between the urban dweller and the farmer which were also reflected in the areas of group identification, social relationships, and cultural behavior. The eventual creation of the large nation meant that people living in areas widely distant from one another would develop regional differences in behavior and self-identification, as well as regionally contained social systems. But most important of all in this connection was the rise of *social classes*. . . .

The significance of social class analysis for our argument is that social classes, though not as precisely bounded as ethnic groups, also become sources of group identification, social areas of confinement for primary group relations, and bearers of particular cultural patterns of behavior. This, in fact, from one point of view, is the most important set of findings which has emerged from the vast accumulation of research and inquiry into social class phenomena in America which social scientists, with accelerating tempo, have been carrying out during the past thirty years. The social class, in other words, while not formally delineated, tends to have its own network of characteristic organizations, institutional activities, and social cliques. These are created because people who are approximately in the same social class have similar interests and tastes, have a common educational background, and work at occupations which bring them in touch with one another in various ways and which involve common types of experience. Thus they feel "comfortable" with each other. These reasons are probably more compelling than sheer "social snobbery" or status consciousness itself in keeping people of widely separated social classes apart from each other in primary group relationships, although doubtless all these reasons interact with one another to produce social separation.

The child, then, grows up in a particular family which is part of a particular class and learns the cultural values of that class as those values are brought home to him in family training, neighborhood play groups, and class-oriented educational patterns. Men of the same social class will thus share certain cultural values and patterns which distinguish them from Americans of other class backgrounds. Upward social mobility, then, involves the need for learning and adopting values and behavior in accordance with the standards of the class into which the upwardly mobile person is moving.

We have now isolated four factors or social categories which play a part in creating subsocieties within the national society that is America. They are ethnic group, social class, rural or urban residence, and region of country lived in. In the original form in which I first published this theory in 1947, my essential thesis was that these four factors do not function in isolation, or serially, but *combine or intersect* to form the basic large social units which make up American society and which bear and transmit the subcultures of America.[6] While the factors are theoretically discrete, they tend to form in their combination *"a functioning unity which has an integrated impact on the participating individual."*[7] Thus a person is not simply a white

Protestant. He is simultaneously a lower-middle class white Protestant living in a small town in the South, or he is an upper-middle class white Catholic living in a metropolitan area in the Northeast, or a lower-class Negro living in the rural South, and so on. To put it in another way, the stratifications based on ethnicity are intersected at right angles by the stratifications based on social class, and the social units or blocks of bounded social space created by their intersection are contained in an urban or a rural setting in a particular region of the country. The analytical scheme is summarized in Table [2].

Table 2. The Subsociety and the Subculture

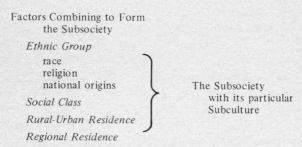

Factors Combining to Form
the Subsociety

Ethnic Group
race
religion
national origins

Social Class

Rural-Urban Residence

Regional Residence

The Subsociety
with its particular
Subculture

Examples of particular subsocieties characterized by particular subcultures:

Upper-middle class white Protestant, southern urban
Lower-middle class white Catholic, northern urban
Lower-lower class Negro Protestant, southern rural
Upper-middle class Negro Protestant, northern urban
Lower-middle class white Jewish, western urban
Upper-class white Jewish, northern urban

Central to this type of analysis is, of course, the relationship of the ethnic group stratification system to the social class stratification system. In 1951 I wrote: "American society is 'criss-crossed' by two sets of stratification structures, one based on social status, economic power, and political power differences, regardless of ethnic background, the other a set of status and power relationships based precisely on division of the population by racial, nationality background, and religious categories into 'Old Americans,' Negroes, Jews,

Catholics, Japanese-Americans, Italians, French-Canadians, etc."[8] In effect, this means that each ethnic group may be thought of as being divided into subgroups on the basis of social class, and that theoretically each ethnic group might conceivably have the whole spectrum of classes within it, although in practice, some ethnic groups will be found to contain only a partial distribution of social class subgroups. . . .

The role of regional and rural-urban factors in contributing to the differential nature of the subsocieties of America is doubtless decreasing with each passing decade, yet they cannot be ruled out entirely in a discussion of this topic even today. The vast differences in the cultural system of white attitudes and behavior toward the Negro which exist between North and South constitute an effective reminder that diversities of geography, climate, and historical experience have placed their respective marks on Americans of various regional localities. . . .

However, these regional differences, along with the differences in way of life between a shrinking rural America and an expanding urban America, are subject to the accelerating onslaught of rapid transportation, mass communications, and the increasing mechanization of a vast array of productive enterprises, including farming. These forces continually narrow the cultural gap between farm and country or Midwest and Far West. Perhaps we can put it this way. In attempting to predict the cultural behavior patterns of any given persons on the basis of the factors making up his subsocietal participation, to know his "region" and whether he is rural or urban (or his position on a scale representing the rural-urban dimension), along with his ethnic group and social class, increases the accuracy of the prediction of his subcultural behavior. However, after one has ascertained his ethnic group and social class, the increase in accuracy of prediction obtained by adding his region and his position on the rural-urban scale is probably not now great, and this increment of predictive accuracy is decreasing with the years. Thus, ethnic group and social class will become increasingly important as the principal background factors making up the subsociety with its subculture in American life.

THE ETHCLASS

If the portion of social space created by the intersection of the ethnic group with the social class is fast becoming the essential form of the subsociety in America, then we need a name for convenient reference to this subsocietal type. I have no great affection for neologisms and am pleased to do without them whenever possible; moreover, the one I am about to suggest has a quality about it which faintly calls to mind the Newspeak of Orwell's society of *1984*. Nevertheless, I have thus tried to disarm my potential critics in advance because the need for some term of reference is great and because the term I am proposing has, at least, the virtues of simplicity and clarity of origin. I propose, then, that we refer to the subsociety created by the intersection of the vertical stratifications of ethnicity with the horizontal stratifications of social class as the *ethclass*. Thus a person's *ethclass* might be upper-middle class white Protestant, or lower-middle class white Irish Catholic, or upper-lower class Negro Protestant, and so on.

We must now inquire into what happens to the three crucial variables of group identity, social participation, and cultural behavior as they pertain to the subsociety of the ethclass, and thus discern how the ethclass functions differentially from the ethnic group itself. I shall offer the following remarks as a set of hypotheses which will be considered in a later chapter in relation to such empirical evidence as is available. These hypotheses apply to American society at mid-century.

1) With regard to cultural behavior, differences of social class are more important and decisive than differences of ethnic group. This means that people of the same social class tend to act alike and to have the same values even if they have different ethnic backgrounds. People of different social classes tend to act differently and have different values even if they have the same ethnic background.

2) With regard to social participation in primary groups and primary relationships, people tend to confine these to their own social class segment within their own ethnic group—that is, to the ethclass.

3) The question of group identification must be dealt with by

distinguishing two types of such identification from one another—one the sense of peoplehood to which we referred earlier, the other a sense of being truly congenial with only a social class segment of that "people." I can best articulate the distinction by quoting in full from one of my previous writings: "The matter of psychological orientations, that is, group identification and patterns of 'in-grouping' and 'out-grouping,' is complicated by the fact that we are dealing here with more than one dimension. Although a person may participate largely in a social field circumscribed by both ethnic group and social class borders, the attribution of ethnic group membership *by itself* is a powerful pattern in our culture—a pattern generated both by pressure from within the ethnic group and from without. Rare is the Negro, or the Jew, for instance, who can fail to respond affectively to events or to evaluative allegations which concern, respectively, Negroes or Jews as a group. Nevertheless, the participation field and the field of close behavioral similarities are likely to be class-confined, as well as ethnic-confined. Thus we may distinguish two types of psychological constellations corresponding to these respective experience patterns. 'I am ultimately bound up with the fate of these people' is the type of constellation attached to the ethnic group as a whole. We may call this *historical identification* since it is a function of the unfolding of past and current historic events. On the other hand, 'These are the people I feel at home with and can relax with' is the type of constellation attached to those persons with whom one participates frequently and shares close behavioral similarities. According to the subcultural hypothesis, these persons are likely to be of the same ethnic group *and* social class (and regional and rural-urban categories). This constellation we may call *participational identification*. To sum up: in terms of psychological orientations, the ethnic group is likely to be the group of historical identification, whereas the subculture [read "ethclass"] will be, in the majority of cases, the group of participational identification. It should be pointed out that identification with larger units—that is, American society as a whole, 'Western society,' 'all humanity,' are likely to be present at different levels of structuring."[9]

Succinctly, then, one may say that the ethnic group is the locus of a sense of *historical identification,* while the ethclass is the locus of a sense of *participational identification*. With a person of the same social class but of a different ethnic group, one shares behavioral similarities but not a sense of peoplehood. With those of the same ethnic group but of a different social class, one shares the sense of peoplehood but not behavioral similarities. The only group which meets both of these criteria are people of the same ethnic group *and* same social class. With these "birds of our feather" we truly share a sense of what the early sociologist, Franklin Giddings, called "consciousness of kind"—with these particular members of the human race and no others we can really relax and participate with ease and without strain.

FOOTNOTES

[1] E. B. Tylor, *Primitive Culture*, London: John Murray, 1891 (third edition), Vol. I, 1. The first edition appeared in 1871.

[2] A further exception should be noted here: the federal government's recognition of religious belief and background as relevant in the case of the conscientious objector to war and military service. Even here, the exemption is not absolute; "alternative service" of a non-military nature is required.

[3] See Paul F. Lazarsfeld, Bernard Berelson, and Hazel Gaudet, *The People's Choice*, New York: Columbia University Press, 1948 (second edition); Bernard R. Berelson, Paul F. Lazarsfeld, and William N. McPhee, *Voting*, Chicago: University of Chicago Press, 1954; Angus Campbell, Gerald Gurin, and Warren E. Miller, *The Voter Decides*, Evanston, Ill.: Row, Peterson and Company, 1954; and Samuel Lubell, *The Future of American Politics*, New York: Doubleday and Co. (Second edition, Doubleday Anchor Books), 1956.

[4] Albert K. Cohen, *Delinquent Boys*, Glencoe, Ill.: The Free Press, 1955. See, also, for such a use of the term, several papers by Alfred McClung Lee: "Levels of Culture as Levels of Social Generalization," *American Sociological Review* (August 1945), 485–95; "Social Determinants of Public Opinions," *International Journal of Opinion and Attitude Research* (March 1947), 12–29; and "A Sociological Discussion of Consistency and Inconsistency in Intergroup Relations," *Journal of Social Issues* (Vol. 5, No. 3), 12–18.

[5] Cf. use of this term in Alfred McClung Lee, "Attitudinal Multivalence in Relation to Culture and Personality," *American Journal of Sociology* (November 1954), 294–9. Lee uses the term to refer to the particularized culture of any group, regardless of scope.

[6] See Milton M. Gordon, "The Concept of the Sub-Culture and Its Application," *Social Forces* (October 1947), 40–42. See, also, "A System of Social Class Analysis," *Drew University Studies*, (August 1951) 15–18; *Social Class in American Sociology*, Durham, N.C.: Duke University Press, 1958, 252–6; and for a fuller exposition, "Social Structure and Goals in Group Relations," in *Freedom and Control in Modern Society*, Morroe Berger, Theodore Abel, and Charles H. Page (eds.), New York: D. Van Nostrand Co.,

1954. In these publications I used the term "subculture" to stand elliptically for both the subsociety and the subculture as defined here.

[7]Gordon, *ibid*. 40 (italics as in original).

[8]Gordon, "A System of Social Class Analysis," *op. cit*., 15–16; see also, *Social Class in American Sociology, op. cit*., 252.

[9]Gordon, "Social Structure and Goals in Group Relations," *op. cit*., 146–7 (italics as in original).

14

NOTES ON THE PRESENT STATUS OF THE CONCEPT SUBCULTURE

John Irwin

The recent emergence of various folk concepts should entice us to re-examine our notion of subculture. I am speaking of such concepts as "scene," "bag," and "thing." The popular use of these indicates that there have been significant shifts in the phenomenon to which subculture refers. Generally, in sociology, subculture has referred to a subset of patterns recognized by social scientists. The use of the metaphors above indicates that it is presently becoming a subset of patterns that the ordinary man recognizes and responds to. This changes the phenomenon in many essential ways, some of which will be discussed in the following paragraphs.[1]

Before turning to the contemporary phenomenon, let me briefly analyze the cognitive status of subculture in its two major uses. In the first systematic definitional treatment of subculture, Milton

Prepared for this volume.

Gordon defines subculture as a subset of cultural patterns carried by a population *segment*.[2] He argues that it would be useful to divide the American society by ethnic, economic, regional and religious variables into segments with unique subcultures. The division into cultural units is somewhat arbitrary, however, since the variables applied do not necessarily relate to other subsystems. These are not necessarily subcultures which are attached to particular social structures or are recognized by anyone except the social scientist applying these variables.[3]

In another of its major uses—subculture as a small group or the patterns carried by a small group—the question of the cognitive status of the concept in the minds of its carriers is likewise ignored. In this version, which traces back to the Chicago deviance studies,[4] but which received its major developments in the 1950's,[5] the problem of whether or not the group which is carrying the subculture or whether a larger group who comes into contact with it recognized the distinct set of patterns is never considered. In fact, in his milestone treatment in *Delinquent Boys*, Cohen seems to assume that the distinct set of patterns does not extend very far. He feels obliged to explain the emergence of each new set of patterns.[6]

SUBCULTURE AS A SOCIAL WORLD

In an early treatment of concepts related to subculture, Tamatsu Shibutani actually supplied a conception of subculture which is highly adaptable to the contemporary phenomenon. He did not, however, use the label. He suggested that *reference groups* should be viewed as *reference worlds*, or *social worlds* which are not tied to any particular collectivity or territory.[7] He also pointed out that persons could simultaneously or alternately identify with more than one social world. Though Shibutani did not call social worlds or reference worlds subcultures, this is one of the ways in which subculture has been viewed. Subculture, rather than the subset of behavior patterns of a segment, or the patterns of a small group, is often thought of as a social world, a shared perspective, which is not attached firmly to any definite group or segment. It is this version which we will adopt here to make sense of contemporary subcultural phenomena in the United States. One dimension of social world as a subculture which Shibutani did not make explicit must be emphasized: The social world can be and often is an explicit category in the minds of a broader population than social scientists and the group carrying the subculture.

SUBCULTURE AS AN EXPLICIT LIFE STYLE

People today are becoming more aware of the existence of subcultures, variant life styles or social worlds, and are more often structuring their own behavior, making decisions and planning future courses of action according to their conception of these explicit subcultural entities. Concrete evidence of this emerging trend is the appearance of several folk metaphors which refer to styles of life as things. The most current of these is the "scene." This metaphor in its present folk usage—such as, in the phrases: "make the scene" and "that's not my scene"—refers mainly to a style of life which is well known among insiders and outsiders to the scene. In the first phrase "make the scene," the scene usually has a definite location and is transitory. It is something which is occuring at a particular time and place. In the second phrase, it refers to a more permanent life style. The usages share three connotations: (1) The style of life is recognized as an explicit and shared category. In other words a particular scene is well known among some relatively large segment. It must be to be a scene, since the term connotes popularity. (2) There are various styles of life available to a particular person, since there is always more than one scene. (3) Finally, one's commitment to a particular scene is potentially tentative and variable.

Two other metaphors which reflect the explicitness of life styles are "bag" and "thing." The phrases "that's not my bag" and "do your own thing," for instance, both reflect that the life styles are being seen as entities.

AMERICAN SUBCULTURAL PLURALISM
AND RELATIVISM

Of course, these metaphors are only used in the daily speech of a small minority. But a larger segment, perhaps a majority, hears them, at least in the mass media, and recognizes their meaning. This is just one indicator that we are generally aware of the "subcultural" pluralism of the American society. Perhaps twenty years ago most people took American culture for granted and assumed that it was the same for everyone (with a few obvious exceptions, of course, such as Indians, foreigners and "deviants").[8] Presently, however, because of the mass media, behavioral scientists' exposes of deviant subcultures, geographical mobility, and higher education, a larger segment of American people have recognized the extent of cultural variation in the country. Accompanying this realization is a shift in one's conception of his own values and beliefs. One may no longer take the "goodness" or the "rightness" of his own culture or subculture for granted. In effect, he is beginning to experience *subcultural relativism.*

SUBCULTURE AS AN ACTION SYSTEM

Increased subcultural pluralism and relativism have effected two important changes in the nature of interaction of the ordinary man. First, one's beliefs, values and cultural meanings have become explicit categories of action. Furthermore, the ordinary man tends to conceive of these categories as a set making up a whole—a life style or cohesive social world. So in a sense persons in interaction are involved in comparing, sharing, negotiating and imparting cultural patterns. While they are doing this they attempt, because of a general human concern for order, to bring the cultural components into a consistent relationship and to maintain boundaries around the system. It may be stated, therefore, that the subculture has become a concrete action system.[9]

BEING ON

The second manner in which interaction is changing is that persons are more often "on." All action categories are becoming more explicit and the person is more often a self conscious *actor*. In an article on the dramaturgic model Sheldon Messinger and others suggested that life is not like a theater.[10] They stated that natural interaction is unselfconscious and the actors did not conceive of themselves as actors in a role. The dramaturgic model is useful, they argue, as an analytical tool, but we must remember that it is seldom a concrete model. They did point out, however, that in some life contexts it approaches concreteness. For instance, the Negro is "on" when he is in the company of whites and the mental patient, who is constantly under the surveillance of judges, is "on" most of the time.

I would like to suggest that with the growing recognition of subcultural pluralism, the increase in subcultural relativism and the emergence of cultural categories as explicit action categories and as a cohesive system, more persons are finding themselves judged by outsiders and finding themselves marginal. They are increasingly "on." They more often see themselves as performers in various "scenes" and are becoming more aware of the dimensions of their various performances. Life is becoming more like a theater.

SUMMARY

In former treatment of the concept subculture the cognitive status of the concept in the minds of the folk was not addressed. This is now highly important because subculture is becoming a conscious category at the folk level. The widespread use of the metaphor "scene" reflects this trend. American people are becoming aware of the subcultural variation in their society and are experiencing subcultural relativism.

This subcultural pluralism and relativism is having two important effects on everyday interaction. One's values, beliefs, and cultural meanings are no longer taken for granted. More often one is involved in consciously comparing, negotiating and sharing these with others.

Furthermore one tends to bring these components into some logically consistent relationship, and therefore, the subculture is becoming an explicit and important action system.

Secondly, action categories in general are becoming more explicit. One is more often conscious of himself as an actor in scenes. Life is becoming more like a theater.

FOOTNOTES

[1]Viewing culture or subculture as explicit categories or as an explicit entity in the minds of the folk sidesteps a particularly troublesome dilemma. This is the problem of circular reasoning in employing culture as an independent variable or explanatory concept. For instance, Edwin Lemert has remarked that "inescapable circularity lies in the use of culture as a summary to describe modal tendencies in the behavior of human beings and, at the same time, as a term of designating the causes of the modal tendencies. The empirically more tenable alternative is that only human beings define, regulate, and control behavior of other human beings." *Human Deviance, Social Problems, and Social Control,* Englewood Cliffs: Prentice-Hall, 1967, 5. But if the folk are making the cultural summary and then defining, regulating and controling behavior of other human beings on the basis of their cultural summary, the concept takes on independence or explanatory weight.

[2]Milton Gordon, "The Concept of the Sub-culture and its Application," *Social Forces* (Oct. 1947), 40–42.

[3]In a later treatment of subculture in his book *Assimilation in American Life* (New York: Oxford University Press, 1964), Milton Gordon relates this use of subculture to "subsociety" which contains "both sexes, all ages, and family groups, and which parallels the larger society in that it provides for a network of groups and institutions extending throughout the individual's entire life cycle." (39) I find these subsocieties to be rather vague entities, however. Some communities and some ethnic segments may take on the dimensions of a subsociety, but many segments which he has designated as carriers of subcultures by his variables do not seem to.

[4]See for instance: Clifford Shaw, *The Jack-Roller,* Chicago: The University of Chicago Press, 1930; Nels Anderson, *The Hobo,* Chicago: University of Chicago Press, 1923; Frederick M. Thrasher, *The Gang,* Chicago: University of Chicago Press, 1927; Clifford Shaw, *The Natural History of a Delinquent Career,* Chicago: University of Chicago Press, 1931; Edwin Sutherland, *The Professional Thief,* Chicago: University of Chicago Press, 1937; and Clifford Shaw, Henry McKay, and James McDonall, *Brothers in Crime,* Chicago: University of Chicago Press, 1938.

[5]See Albert Cohen, *Delinquent Boys,* Glencoe, Ill: The Free Press, 1955; Richard A. Cloward and Lloyd Ohlin, *Delinquency and Opportunity,* Glencoe, Ill: The Free Press, 1960; and Howard S. Becker, *Outsiders,* Glencoe, Ill: The Free Press, 1963.

[6]See Albert Cohen, op. cit., chap. III.

[7]Tamotsu Shibutani, "Reference Groups as Perspectives," *American Journal of Sociology* (1955), 562–569.

[8]The belief in the consensus of American values and beliefs was reflected in R. K. Merton's theory of *anomie* introduced in 1938. Merton suggested at that time that Americans generally shared the same "culturally defined goals, purposes and interests." ("Social Structure and Anomie," *American Sociological Review,* Oct., 1938, 673) It is also revealing that in the 1950's and 60's this assumption in his theory is one which has been most often questioned. For instance, see Edwin Lemert, "Social Structure, Social Control and Deviation," in Marshal Clinard, ed., *Anomie and Deviant Behavior,* New York: The Free Press of Glencoe, 1964, 64–71.

[9]In a collective statement as an introduction to *Toward A General Theory of Action,* (New York: Harper & Row, 1951, 7), Talcott Parsons, Edward A. Shils, Gordon W. Allport, Clyde Kluckhohn, Henry A. Murray, Robert R. Sears, Richard C. Sheldon, Samuel A. Stouffer, and Edward C. Tolman write that "the cultural tradition in its significance both as an *object* of orientation and as an *element* in the orientation of action must be articulated both conceptually and empirically with personalities and social systems. Apart from embodiment in the orientation systems of concrete actors, culture, though existing as a body of artifacts and as systems of symbols, is not in itself organized as a system of action."

[10]"Life as a Theater: Some Notes on the Dramaturgic Approach to Social Reality," *Sociometry* (March, 1962).

SUGGESTIONS FOR FURTHER READING

David J. Bordua, "Delinquent Subcultures: Sociological Interpretations of Gang Delinquency," *Annals of the American Academy of Political and Social Science*, vol. 338 (Nov., 1961), pp. 119-136.

Richard A. Cloward and Lloyd E. Ohlin, *Delinquency and Opportunity*, New York: The Free Press (1960).

William J. Goode, "Community Within a Community: The Professions," *American Sociological Review*, vol. 22, no. 2 (April, 1957), pp. 194-200.

Charles Kadushin, "The Friends and Supporters of Psychotherapy: On Social Circles in Urban Life," *American Sociological Review*, vol. 31, no. 6 (Dec., 1966), pp. 786-802.

Charles Kadushin, "Power, Influence and Social Circles: A New Methodology for Studying Opinion Makers," *American Sociological Review*, vol. 33, no. 5 (Oct., 1968), pp. 685-699.

Fred E. Katz, "Occupational Contact Networks," *Social Forces*, vol. 37, no. 1, (Oct., 1958), pp. 52-55.

John I. Kitsuse and David C. Dietrich, "Delinquent Boys: A Critique," *American Sociological Review*, vol. 24, no. 2 (April, 1959), pp. 208-215.

Alfred McClung Lee, "Attitudinal Multivalence in Relation to Culture and Personality," *American Journal of Sociology*, vol. 60, no. 3 (Nov., 1954), pp. 294-299.

Norton E. Long, "The Local Community as an Ecology of Games," *American Journal of Sociology*, vol. 64, no. 3 (Nov., 1958), pp. 251-261.

David Matza, *Delinquency and Drift*, New York: John Wiley & Sons (1964).

Tamotsu Shibutani, "Reference Groups as Perspectives," *American Journal of Sociology*, vol. 60 (May, 1955), pp. 562-569.

Gresham M. Sykes and David Matza, "Techniques of Neutralization: A Theory of Delinquency," *American Sociological Review*, vol. 22, no. 5 (Oct., 1957), pp. 664-670.

THE GLENDESSARY PRESS
2490 Channing Way
Berkeley, California 94704